T0383479

SECRETS OF THE
BARN FIND HUNTER

THE ART OF FINDING
LOST COLLECTOR CARS

TOM COTTER
INTRODUCTION BY McKEEL HAGERTY

motorbooks

Inspiring | Educating | Creating | Entertaining

Brimming with creative inspiration, how-to projects, and useful information to enrich your everyday life, Quarto.com is a favorite destination for those pursuing their interests and passions.

© 2022 Quarto Publishing Group USA Inc.
Text © 2022 Tom Cotter

First Published in 2022 by Motorbooks, an imprint of The Quarto Group,
100 Cummings Center, Suite 265-D, Beverly, MA 01915, USA.
T (978) 282-9590 F (978) 283-2742 Quarto.com

Motorbooks titles are also available at discount for retail, wholesale, promotional, and bulk purchase. For details, contact the Special Sales Manager by email at specialsales@quarto.com or by mail at The Quarto Group, Attn: Special Sales Manager, 100 Cummings Center, Suite 265-D, Beverly, MA 01915, USA.

26 25 24 23 22   1 2 3 4 5

ISBN: 978-0-7603-7297-5

Digital edition published in 2022
eISBN: 978-0-7603-7298-2

Library of Congress Cataloging-in-Publication Data available

Design: Cindy Samargia Laun
Cover Image: Jordan Lewis
Photography: Courtesy of Tom Cotter, unless otherwise noted.

Printed in China

DEDICATION

Dedicated to Woody, the man, not the car. Woody was my traveling companion on so many great road trips. RIP, Woodman.

ACKNOWLEDGEMENTS

Lots of folks helped make this book a reality. If I leave you out, please don't be upset, but the ones I can recall include alphabetically:

Larry Bauer, Ritchie Clyne, Brian Cotter, Matt DeGarmo, Tony Giordano, Geoff Hacker, David Hinton, Jay Leno, Jordan Lewis, Kevin Mackay, Jim Maxwell, Bob Meade, Tom Miller, Janice Lee Moskowitz, Mark Moskowitz, Michael Alan Ross, Pat Ryan, Tom Shaughnessy, Chuck Schoendorf, Tim Suddard, and Bill Warner. Additionally, a big thanks to my publisher, Zack Miller, who is always willing to listen to my crazy book ideas. And finally, my wife, Pat, who does (most of) the housework, yard work, Holiday decorating, and so on while I bang away on my keyboard.

INTRODUCTION
BY McKEEL HAGERTY * 6

PROLOGUE
THE GATEWAY DRUG TO THE OLD CAR HOBBY * 10

McKeel Hagerty still enjoying the Porsche 911 he and his father restored four decades earlier.

INTRODUCTION

By McKeel Hagerty

I am perhaps one of the few people whose barn find journey began as early in life as Tom Cotter's.

As Tom describes in the wonderful and witty book that you are about to enjoy, his journey began when he was a lad of twelve and fell in love with an abandoned late 1950s Fiat 1100 sedan that he spotted at the end of a dead-end street. He and his brother Rob dragged it home, thus unwittingly setting himself on a path to future YouTube (and book-writing) glory.

My first and best barn find came when I was thirteen. My dad, a life-long tinkerer and car guy, had a deal with his son and two daughters as we approached our driving years: We could each have a car, but it had to be a used one and we had to fix it up with him. It sounded like a great deal to me! After months of searching, we ultimately found the car that would become my first—a rusted-out 1967 Porsche 911S—in not one, but two Michigan snow-banks behind an old barn belonging to a crusty body shop owner who had ice-raced the 911 to death on weekends. One snowbank held the body, the other the engine, which he had removed to fix up "someday." (As Tom relates in the book, "I can't sell it because I'm going to fix it up someday!" is a phrase he's heard a thousand times from car owners who: Just. Can't. Let. Go.)

In the case of the 911's owner, "someday" was clearly never going to come, so he sold it to me for 500 bucks. It would take dad and me two years to reunite the body with the engine and get it running again, and it would be years more before it was professionally restored and became the car that it is today. But, boy, was the effort worth it. To this day, that little car (once black, now red) is the first I take out of the garage in the spring and the last I put away for the winter. The memory of finding it and then piecing it back together with my dad makes it far more valuable than any other car I'll ever own, bar none.

That's the funny thing about these hunks of metal, rubber, and glass that we all love so much: It's the stories and memories associated with them—not as much the cars themselves—that in the end matter most. Tom's show, *Barn Find Hunter*, is built on that alchemy. There's an undeniable and indefinable allure—and a great story—behind every barn find, whether it results in a purchase or not. It's the thrill of the hunt combined with the search for buried treasure that appeals to the car-kid within each of us, whether it's us doing the hunting or Tom and his film crew.

Direct or vicarious, we are lucky for such experiences. Aside from my 911S, I've had several other barn find adventures. I'll relate just one. Out of the blue, apropos of nothing, a friend one day said rather casually, "Hey, I hear there might be an old E-Type in a barn near here. Do you wanna go check it out?" I chuckled because that was a rhetorical question if ever I'd heard one, and he knew it. To a car collector, the prospect of an E-Type sitting alone—and possibly available—in a barn somewhere is like an old pirate in stories of yore handing you a map and asking if you want to sail off in search of buried treasure: OF COURSE you do!

(BELOW LEFT)
Thirteen-year-old McKeel posing with the Porsche 911 that would soon to be his.

(BELOW RIGHT)
Retrieving the six-cylinder engine that was conveniently stored under a snowbank near the 911.

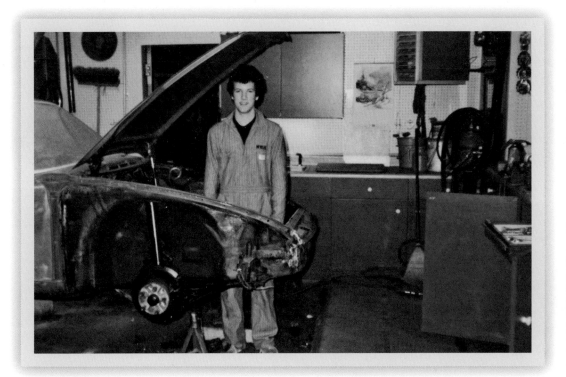

Frank, the senior Hagerty, required each of his three children to spend time with him in the garage, learning skills that would help them throughout their lives. Here McKeel is about to learn the art of welding.

So, that's exactly what we did. Frankly, I expected the barn to be empty. I've been around the block enough times to know that many would-be barn finds turn out to be vapor. But when we arrived, sure enough, there it was under a thick layer of dust—an honest-to-gosh original-condition 1966 Jaguar E-Type with 13,000 miles on it that hadn't been driven in twenty-eight years. Wow! Long story short, I bought it from the owner, fixed it up, and drive it to this day. I never did find out why the car ended up in that barn in the first place—did it break down and the owner couldn't find the parts to fix it? Was it just not his cup of tea? Did he inherit it from a relative and simply had no interest in it? The backstory, as anyone who watches *Antiques Roadshow*, *American Pickers*, or *Barn Find Hunter* knows, is often the most interesting part of a find, so I should have thought to ask—rookie mistake. Clearly, I'm no Tom Cotter. Then again, who is? Here's a man who has spent a lifetime honing the automotive, investigatory, and people skills it takes to make a show like *Barn Find Hunter* seem easy when, I assure you, it is not.

If, like me, you admire Tom and his work, strap in because you're in for a fun ride within the pages of *Secrets of the Barn Find Hunter*. You will discover no less than everything you ever want to know about the fine art of unearthing old cars—from the inside story of how the *Barn Find Hunter* series came to be to Tom's wildest stories and biggest screwups.

The following story is not among those wild tales, but it is one my favorite stories from Tom's show. You may remember it. In Episode 46, titled "The Greatest Barn Find Collection Known to Man," Tom is in his pickup negotiating a slick, muddy, dead-end road through a tunnel of trees in the middle of nowhere on his way to see a man named Billy. Of that road, Tom says, "No one wants to go down dead-end roads, but that's where the treasure is." It's fantastic advice for both finding cars and for life, really.

Billy, it turns out, is a kindly, older gent who collected and restored a lot of cars thirty to forty years ago, so long ago that some of them are in the slow process of unrestoring themselves with the help of Mother Nature. Tom is hopeful he'll be able to buy something from the hundreds of cars in Billy's possession: Dodge Daytonas, a Plymouth Superbird, big block Chevys, Ford Thunderbirds, an L-82 Corvette with under ten miles, a De Tomaso Pantera, even Billy's high school car, a 1958 Chrysler Imperial. But it's a no-go. Billy's not selling, but no matter. If you know Tom, you know he wasn't disappointed, any more than a deer hunter who doesn't bag a buck considers the hunt a failure. It's the journey, after all, not the destination. There are always more barns to hunt in Tom's world.

And we, my friends, get to tag along.

Lucky us.

McKeel Hagerty is CEO at Hagerty Group, LLC.

Of all the cars in his garage, the Porsche McKeel restored as a teenager with his Dad means the most to him.

PROLOGUE:

THE GATEWAY DRUG TO THE OLD CAR HOBBY

I didn't invent the term *barn find*, but it's a brilliant catchall phrase to identify a neglected car that might be sitting in a barn; or a warehouse; or a field, garage, carport, driveway, backyard, parking lot, or just about anyplace else. Word is that about ten years ago, one of the big auction houses tried to trademark the term "Barn Find," probably hoping to cash in by licensing it to users. Thankfully, their request was denied because it had already become part of the American nomenclature. And thank goodness, because it's just too healthy and descriptive to lock away or charge those who desire to use it.

So, whoever invented the term, thank you.

I've been looking for old cars since I was a kid—like twelve- or thirteen-years old, probably earlier. But I never thought about it as a career option. Looking for "sheds" was a secret obsession; one I didn't think anyone else shared. Here's a long story explaining how I came to realize I was not alone in my quest for vintage tin . . .

Ever since I was ten-years-old, I had dreamed of one day owning a genuine 289 Cobra. The problem was that because of the cars' ever-increasing value, I thought my disposable income would never ever catch up. But the stars aligned with the sale of my business, and I was actually in a financial position to consider becoming the owner of a real small-block Cobra.

The one I decided on was CSX2490, meaning it was the 490th Cobra built.

(**Quick Cobra History Lesson:** What does CSX mean? Most assume it stands for **C**arroll **S**helby e**X**port, but that is not entirely correct. AC Cars (originally called Auto Carriers, Ltd.), the English auto manufacturer contracted to manufacture the base vehicle for Carroll Shelby's sports car, designated the Cobra with the prefix "C" because it was the third model derivative of their "Ace" model; the "S" stood for Shelby; "X" denoted export cars with left-hand drive; the numeral "2" designated cars with small-block engines (a "3" would later designate big-block cars); and the three numerals that followed designated the sequential serial number of each car: for example, Carroll Shelby's first prototype was CSX2000, the first production Cobra was CSX2001, and so on. The car I fell in love with was the 490th Cobra. This lesson will come in handy if you stumble across a Cobra in a barn . . .).

Anyway, it was a great car and just what I had dreamed about since fifth grade: painted wire wheels, no roll bar, no side pipes, just a plain-Jane Cobra. The car was located in Walnut Creek, California, in the San Francisco Bay Area, and I lived in North Carolina. Instead of having it shipped, I decided to drive it home cross-country.

I invited my friend Peter Egan, then editor-at-large at *Road & Track* magazine, to join me as codriver. We had a blast, driving secondary roads all the way across the United States over the course of nine days. Peter wrote a great story about our adventure that appeared in *Road & Track*'s February 2002 issue. You can find it online with a search for "Cross Country Cobra."

OPPOSITE: This was a sad discovery on the Maine coast: a Jaguar E-Type Series One, crashed in the 1970s and then covered with heavy plastic tarp for forty years. When finally uncovered, the totally rotted car sold for $10,000. *Tom Cotter*

After dreaming about Cobra ownership since fifth grade, the stars aligned in the year 2000 and I was able to actually purchase one. The resulting story in *Road & Track* resulted in my "discovering" a similar car in my neighbor's barn, eleven books about barn finds, and the *Barn Find Hunter* YouTube series. *Tom Cotter*

Soon after the article appeared, I received a call from a neighbor whom I had never met. "Hello, Tom, this is Hugh Barger, your neighbor," he said. "I own Barger Farm." Hugh owns a 500-acre farm about a half-mile from my house, and I actually share a fence line with him.

"I just read the story about your AC Cobra and really enjoyed it," Barger said. "I'd like to see it in person, and I'd like to show you what I have in my barn . . ."

I was all ears. At that point, I had driven past Hugh's barn for more than a decade, always wondering if there might be something interesting inside. Having snooped inside hundreds of barns in my life, though, I can verify that most old barns have old tractors or piles of hay, seldom cars.

So, what was inside Hugh's barn?

The following Saturday, my son Brian and I drove the Cobra up the long driveway to Hugh's house. He admired our recently acquired car and admitted that he had wanted a Cobra since he was a young man. He told me he even communicated with the AC factory in the late 1970s about having them build him a Cobra, but he said the cost was prohibitive. Eventually, he invited us into the barn to see his car. There, parked for at least thirty years at the time, was an AC Greyhound, an aluminum-bodied, Bristol-powered coupe that rolled off the same assembly line in Thames Ditton, England, as my Cobra—just a half-mile from my house!

How could this be? I was amazed.

Arriving back home, an hour later, my editor at Motorbooks, Lee Klancher, happened to call. We had been talking regularly about another book project since I had written *Holman-Moody: The Legendary Race Team*, several years earlier.

"You'll never guess what just happened," I said. I went on to explain that my neighbor had an AC Greyhound, just a half-mile from my own home where I garaged my AC Cobra.

"Tom," Lee said, "that's it!"

I asked, "What's it?"

"Your next book, *The Cobra in the Barn*," he said. "A book about barn find cars."

I was a little confused. Understand, this was twenty years ago, and the term *barn find* was barely on anybody's radar.

"Really?," I asked. "Do you think anybody will actually be interested in a book about finding old cars?"

Lee believed enthusiasts would be interested in reading about how interesting cars are discovered.

The result was *The Cobra in the Barn*, the first of ten books I've written on the subject. (This book makes 11.) It's a best seller, which in the car book category, is saying something.

So, as it turned out, I was not the only person interested in learning about, and reading about, old car discoveries—barn finds. That book seemed to open the floodgates, resulting in books by other authors, magazine columns, websites, and eventually a phone call from Hagerty.

"Is this Tom Cotter?" asked Clair Walters.

"Yes," I replied.

"We at Hagerty like your books and think the concept might work well in a video format," she said. "Would you be open to that?"

I agreed and we filmed a pilot program, which seemed to work. Six years later and *Barn Find Hunter*, which airs every two weeks, has more than one million subscribers.

I DIDN'T INVENT THE TERM BARN FIND, BUT IT'S A BRILLIANT CATCHALL PHRASE.

The car that started it all: my series of barn find books, the *Barn Find Hunter* video series, and who knows how many other "Picker" shows. It's an AC Greyhound and was built in the same English factory that build my own AC Cobra. The car has not moved since the 1970s and still sits in a barn just one-half mile from my house in North Carolina. *Jordan Lewis*

Before we get into the meat of the book, here are a couple of my barn find rules:

1. I'm regularly scolded on social media for identifying a car as a barn find only to be told, "No, it can't be—it's not in a barn." I try to ignore these comments. I have probably used the term more than anyone over the past couple of decades, so I feel safe in taking liberties with its definition. If anyone gives you a hard time for using it, tell them I said it was okay.

2. I often see cars on social media referred to as "abandoned." If a car is truly abandoned, then you should be able to take it for free. It was junked! It has no owner. However, if it's on private property, it's not actually abandoned—it's just a barn find (see above).

Enjoy the ride!

1
COLLECTOR-CAR
COLD
CALLING

Will Rogers sagely noted "You never get a second chance to make a good first impression."

When I parked in front of David Shoemaker's house, I thought, "Jeez, I could be shot."

While searching for cars in West Virginia for a book titled *Barn Find Road Trip*, a repair shop owner in the little town of Keyser said there was an old fellow up in the hills who had a bunch of old cars. Craig Boddy, owner of Boddy's Automotive, told me David Shoemaker's house was just off Fried Meat Ridge Road.

"Go see David," he said.

Fried Meat Ridge Road? Obviously, we were not in Kansas anymore.

I was born and raised near New York City, and most of what I knew about the rural South was gleaned from the movie *Deliverance*. So, driving up a country road in West Virginia to meet a mountain man got my attention and not in the best way. Cue "Dueling Banjos."

Having spent more than half a century searching for old cars, I guess I should count my blessings that I've never been shot. In all those years, I've been threatened by hundreds of dogs, but thanks to chains and fences, I've only been bitten once. I've been cussed at and chased off property, but thankfully, the only blood I have shed was the result of barbed wire, thorn bushes, or rusty fenders.

(Actually, I have a six-inch scar on my thigh from a time in my reckless youth when I went looking for old cars in a Riverhead, New York, junkyard while barefoot and wearing shorts!)

Here's Pro-Tip #1—Keep your tetanus shot current!

I am always careful and *almost* never break the law while searching for old cars on private property. After decades of knocking on doors, I have developed a certain schtick, a technique. But before I departed on my *Barn Find Road Trip*, I had never hunted for cars in West Virginia, where friends warned me to be careful when approaching hollers and hillbillies. So, I was nervous about going off the beaten path into "them thar hills."

Once I turned off Fried Meat Ridge Road onto Dry Creek Road, it was obvious where Shoemaker lived. There were old cars scattered in front and beside his house and along the road. There was an assortment of old Fords and Chevies and a 1940 Chrysler three-window coupe. A Model A Roadster was actually parked on the roof of his shop!

I parked "Woody", my 1939 Ford Deluxe wagon, in front of the tidy house and surveyed my surroundings. (The Ford is my barn find hunting vehicle of choice. Fifty years ago, it was a barn find itself. It was owned by a Long Island surfer when I stumbled across it at fifteen-years-old. I bought it for $300, and I still drive it as often as I can.) The place was rural, for sure, but not threatening. I got out and walked toward the house. A dog— a brown, medium-sized junkyard variety—jumped out from behind the bushes, showed his teeth, and began to bark loudly. I decided to backtrack to my car and escape, if the dog and my feet would let me. Just then, a woman

Initially, I was nervous about approaching the rural home in West Virginia, but owner David Shoemaker was one of the nicest old car enthusiasts I've ever met. He gave us full run of his property to photograph any of the dozens of cars he owned. *Michael Alan Ross*

came to the front door, looked at my car, and said, "Oh, you must be looking for David. He's working on a bulldozer up the mountain." Then, thankfully, she called off the dog.

She introduced herself as Shirley, David's wife. She looked like the kind of woman who made amazing chocolate chip cookies.

"Should I come back later?" I asked.

"No, he'll be right down," she said. "I'm sure he heard the dog barking, which means he knows someone is here. But you can look around in the meantime."

That was easier than I thought. Just as I started to walk toward the old Chrysler three-window coupe, a ragtag pickup truck drove up and an old fellow got out. He introduced himself as David and we shook hands.

His hands were large, powerful, and calloused, like someone whose livelihood has relied on them his whole life. David Shoemaker was a mountain man, but rather than threatening, I could tell he was a gentle soul.

His face told the story of living on the mountain for seven decades. Harsh winters and hot summers were etched into the creases that crossed his cheeks. His short, scrubby beard, now all the rage with twenty-somethings, is what mountain men have been wearing in West Virginia for centuries. My photographer, Michael Alan Ross, was fascinated by the character of David's face and later told me he could have photographed his portrait all afternoon.

David turned out to be one of the nicest people I've met in all my years of barn find hunting. He was friendly, accommodating, and even offered us iced tea, the ultimate Southern compliment. He told us a short version of his life story, including that he had settled here on the creek when he got married in 1958 and that his daughter shared his love of working on cars. He gave me free rein of his property to look at all of his cars.

One of the more interesting cars in Shoemaker's yard was this 1941 Chrysler 3-window coupe. He said that President Franklin Delano Roosevelt owned two just like it: the serial number in front and behind this car's number. His plan had been to install a Hemi engine in it, but said he would sell the car. *Michael Alan Ross*

I asked if he would be willing to sell any of them, expecting the standard answer of, "No!"

"Well, I'm getting older, and my health is not the best," he said, "so it's a good time to let some of them go."

I've met hundreds of David Shoemakers in my life and am thankful each time because enthusiasts like him are the salt of the earth and only want to tell their story. These people collectively own tens of thousands of the cars we call barn finds. They are the gatekeepers who potentially hold your key to vintage car ownership, possibly at bargain-basement prices. But how you conduct yourself during what I term the "cold call" period could spell the difference between success and failure in purchasing an old car.

H unting for old cars has gotten harder in recent years. When I started, many people genuinely wanted to get rid of the cars that littered their yards, carports, and driveways. My first purchase, at fourteen-years-old, was a 1940 Ford Deluxe convertible that sat behind Charlie's Welding Shop on Route 25A in Rocky Point on Long Island.

"Sure, twenty five bucks," Charlie said when I inquired about the car, painted in what seemed to be a variety of household primer paint colors mostly in the black, blue, and red palettes.

I couldn't believe my luck. I had been an enthusiast for that model convertible ever since seeing Clarence "Lumpy" Rutherford, the neighborhood bully, driving one on *Leave it to Beaver*. The car on the show had just the right look: sleek lines and styling that bridged the prewar styling of 1930s cars and the more modern postwar cars.

The car behind Charlie's, though, didn't look quite as sleek. The dash gauges were missing, as were the seats—and the floors. But the stainless steel side molding, even though mostly painted with the various colors of primer, were still attached and in good shape.

And, there was an attractive exterior mirror mounted on the left-side cowl, which got my attention.

I had twenty-five dollars saved from my paper route, so the purchase price wasn't an issue. But suddenly I was broke, and Charlie's Welding Shop was about thirty miles from our home. I convinced a towing company to transport the car for twenty-five bucks, which my mother loaned me. These days, twenty-five dollars will get you a large Growler of good craft-brewed beer, but in 1968, twenty-five dollars would buy my family's groceries for the week. Still, I promised my mom I'd pay her back, and within a day, the car was sitting in our yard.

At fourteen-years-old, I became a Tom Sawyer of sorts, convincing friends to help me remove the paint from my first barn find, a 1940 Ford Deluxe convertible, purchased for twenty-five dollars. It resembled the car Norman "Lumpy" Rutherford drove on the TV show, *Leave it to Beaver*. I sold it when I purchased my 1939 Ford Woody a year later. *Tom Cotter*

It was a big deal in my neighborhood. Everyone knew Tommy Cotter was a car nut—what with all the wooden coaster karts my friends and I had built and raced down the hill on Avenue C—but this would be Tommy's first real car.

Friends came over and helped me sand off the old paint and apply spray cans of new primer. It was what we kids did that summer and after school in the fall.

I read *Rod & Custom* magazine religiously, so I knew exactly how I wanted the car to look: dark Navy Blue metallic, saddle leather interior, 283 cubic inch Chevy engine. The only problem was, I didn't have a dime. I did have a pink Volkswagen Karman-Ghia, though, and an older kid on Avenue B said he would trade a 283 engine he had for the Ghia.

The kid—I forget his name—came with a couple of friends and pushed the non-running Ghia home. In turn, my brother Rob and I tried to push the Chevy V-8 engine on a chopped-down shopping cart the several blocks home. But it was summer, and the asphalt streets were as soft as a marshmallow, which meant the shopping cart's wheels were sinking. The seemingly simple job took many frustrating hours.

(If I hadn't mentioned it before, thanks for helping, Rob.)

Eventually, as neighborhood kids began joining Little League baseball teams, work on the convertible ground to a halt. I began to lose interest, especially when I discovered a 1939 Ford Deluxe Woody Wagon in much better condition. I decided to break the car up for parts.

I sold the trim, fenders, hood, and trunk and easily made my money back. And the mirror—remember the attractive cowl-mounted mirror that was mounted on the car? It turns out it was a rare item, and I was offered $125.

All-in-all, I made several hundred dollars on that old Ford, which left a positive impression on me to continue wheeling and dealing in old cars.

After decades of approaching strangers about their old cars, I have developed a specific attitude: all Car Guys and Car Girls are friends, but some of us just haven't met yet.

I, a perfect stranger, can approach another car person who has entirely different tastes in automobiles, and within just a few minutes, we're like best friends. It's an amazing transformation that takes authenticity to achieve. A poseur is easily identified and turned away. But a real car person, one who is a student of the hobby, is appreciated even by a perfect stranger.

We all like to make new friends, and when a potential new friend comes knocking on the door, it's an exciting moment. Our new pal could be someone to have coffee with, someone to assist with a project, or someone who might be able to provide needed parts. But really, just talking to another enthusiast is reward enough, especially if they live a long way off.

When I'm driving my Woody, with its 1939 North Carolina license plates, in California, or Texas, or Iowa, it always spurs conversation about how the old car hobby is doing "Back East." When we shot *Barn Find Hunter* episodes in Alaska, I made all sorts of friends who wanted to learn about the hobby "down in the States." For my part, I wanted to learn about how they enjoyed their race cars and street rods in Alaska where the driving season is but four months long.

WOULDN'T IT BE NICE IF CAR GUYS AND CAR GALS COULD BECOME INTERNATIONAL DIPLOMATS? THE WORLD MIGHT BE A MORE FRIENDLY PLACE.

OFTEN IT TAKES A COOL OLD CAR
TO FIND COOL OLD CARS . . .

Imagine this: You spot a cool old car partially hidden in the carport of a home as you drive through a rural area. As you pass, your mind is racing at the speed of a mainframe supercomputer, "Wow, I would like to own that car, but my wife will kill me, I don't have any money, my garage is filled to the rafters, I have nine projects already underway," etc. But after a thirty second analysis, you have figured out how to justify it. You make a U-turn, make a beeline back to the house, and turn your shiny new SUV into the driveway.

You stroll up to the door and knock.

"Excuse me, is the XYZ Super Sport in your carport for sale?" you ask.

The man, somewhat elderly, looks at you and then looks at your freshly polished $60,000 SUV parked in his driveway.

"No, I'm going to fix it one day," And the door closes, literally and figuratively.

In less than three minutes, you're back on the road wondering how the outcome could somehow have been different.

Possibly the world's best ice breaker, my 1939 Ford has opened many doors that normally would have remained shut. I bought it as a fifteen-year-old for $300. I find that women are most attracted to the car because it resembles a nice piece of furniture. *Michael Alan Ross*

Here's my second favorite "welcome wagon," the 1967 Ford Country Squire I found during a barn find hunting trip in Michigan. It's the only wagon produced that year with a 428 cubic inch engine, a four-speed transmission, bucket seats, and a console. People who saw it either thought I was the coolest dude in the world or was homeless. *Jordan Lewis*

I have one solution: drive something cool. Make the car you park in the driveway at least as interesting as the one you are inquiring about.

My 1939 Ford Woody and until recently, my '67 Ford Country Squire, have become those vehicles. I call them my icebreakers—my "welcome wagons."

When the old guy looks out to his driveway and sees my car, the response usually is, "Let me get my shoes on. I'll be right out." That's because he wants to see my car as badly as I want to see his! You show me yours, and I'll show you mine! Suddenly, we're on equal turf. He understands that I'm not a poseur or someone who just might want to pick up his car cheap and flip it for a big profit.

I realize that not all of my readers have a 1939 Ford Woody Wagon or a patinated, 428-powered, four-speed Ford Country Squire in their fleet, but the point is, if you have an interesting old car, drive it when searching for old cars.

The mere fact that you are driving an interesting car gives you instant street cred. You get it. You are part of the old car fraternity.

Plus, because older vintage cars attract attention wherever they go, there is always a chance someone will strike up a conversation, which could lead to another old car tip. It happens at gas stations, restaurants, hotels, auto parts stores, even the frozen custard stand. (BTW, I love frozen custard.) Everybody wants to talk about the good old days when their mother drove them to school in an identical car.

An older, interesting car is your calling card and can generate curiosity even from blocks away. I have yet to be turned down or ignored when I've parked my Woody in someone's driveway.

If you can, give it a try.

CUNNINGHAM C-3

I was invited by my friend John Finger to be the keynote speaker at the Central Carolina's Chapter of the Sports Car Club of America 2008 annual awards banquet. Of course, my topic was barn finds. When I was finished with my slide presentation and talk, I sat down at the table to eat my rubber chicken. But before I take a bite, my friend John, one of my table mates, asked me a question that I am often asked.

"What would be your ultimate barn find?"

I explained that for most of my life, I had hoped to find a 289 Cobra, a car I had desired since fifth grade. But I had already found one of those—in a barn in Indianapolis—and bought it and restored it. So, I had fulfilled that automotive fantasy.

John then asked me a follow-up question, which had never happened before, and, in some ways, changed my life. "What would be your SECOND ultimate barn find?" I had to think for a moment.

For much of my adult life, I've been intrigued by sportsman and racer Briggs Cunningham, who built and raced Chrysler Hemi-powered sports cars in an attempt to win the 24 Hours of Le Mans in the 1950s. But before his cars could compete there, he had to homologate them by becoming a bona fide automobile manufacturer like Jaguar, Ferrari, Aston Martin, and others. Cunningham never wanted to build street cars, but rules are rules, so he became the reluctant manufacturer of twenty-five Continentals, or

My favorite barn find ever is the Hemi-powered 1952 Cunningham C-3 Vignale coupe that I found in the basement of an industrial building in Greenville, South Carolina. One of only twenty-five built, I had dreamed of owning one for decades. Finding it was the greatest stroke of luck in my car-hunting career. *Dom Milano*

This is the same car when new in 1952 at the Watkins Glen Concours d'Elegance, where it won its class. Briggs Cunningham built twenty-five Hemi-powered chassis in Florida that were then shipped to Turin, Italy, where they were fitted with an aluminum body by Vignale. To find one that had been sitting for fifty years was a stroke of luck. *Harold Lance*

C-3s, twenty coupes, and five convertibles. The rolling chassis, powered by Hemi engines, were fabricated at the B.S. Cunningham Company factory in West Palm Beach, Florida. The completed chassis were then shipped to Turin, Italy, where Giovanni Michelotti–designed aluminum bodies were installed by Vignale.

For decades, I had collected everything I could find about Cunninghams: books, artwork, toys—I even met Mr. Cunningham himself at his museum in the early 1980s—but came to the realization that actually owning a Cunningham car was something I would likely never achieve.

"My second ultimate barn find would be a Cunningham," I told John and the rest of the guests at the table, who were now all listening. "But there were only twenty-five ever built, and I'm sure they are all owned by millionaire car collectors."

"I know where a Cunningham is," John said without missing a beat. "It's in Greenville."

I was floored. How could this be? I was in Spartanburg, South Carolina, and I'm being told there is a Cunningham just south of where I'm sitting? I surmised that it was likely a fiber-glass-bodied kit car—a clone—that resembled a Cunningham. Yeah, and it probably had a Corvair engine. No way could it be real . . .

"A friend of mine owns it. I can take you there next week."

Next week couldn't come fast enough. I met John in Greenville at his Mazda dealership and then followed him to the industrial building that apparently housed the Cunningham.

Let me say a few things about John. He is a looong-time sports car racer, having competed in an anemic 850 cc Mini in the very first Sports Car Club of America (SCCA) Trans-Am race held at Sebring in 1966. He's raced in everything from Bugeye Sprites to NASCAR Cup cars. He also holds the ultimate speed record for the Chimney Rock Hill Climb, set in a turbocharged, Mazda rotary-powered "wing on wheels." Plus, he owns the Mazda dealership. So, this guy is cars 24/7/365.

John introduced me to the Cunningham's owner, Sam, and we all stepped into the building. Both Sam and John must have been amused by my gushing enthusiasm the moment I laid eyes on the Cunningham, completely ignoring the Lamborghini Miura parked next to it. The C-3 was real. Sam explained that even though he was not a serious Cunningham enthusiast, his father had been, so when this one became available locally, he bought it in memory of his dad. He had purchased the car ten or fifteen years earlier and quickly told me he was not interested in selling it.

The car was rough, a true barn find, which didn't scare me. Thankfully, it was complete. I gave the car a quick inspection and pleaded with Sam to let me purchase the car if he ever changed his mind. We parted on good terms with Sam inviting me to come back to further investigate the car anytime.

One year went by, then two, but I always stayed in touch and even visited once or twice. One time I actually asked if I could purchase fifty percent of the car, so that I could refurbish the mechanicals and begin enjoying it. He turned down my offer, but soon after Sam called and said he had a change of heart.

"You are the right guy to own that car," he said. "Nobody has ever shown as much enthusiasm about that car as you. Come on down and let's do a deal."

The moral of the story? Even cars that are not for sale are eventually sold. You have to sell yourself to the owner before you can buy a car. Salesmanship is required on both sides of a transaction, especially if you have a reluctant seller.

If I had pressured Sam or lowballed him with a cheap offer, he likely would have sold it to someone else. Instead, I showed Sam that I was a sincere buyer who would not flip the car to another buyer, but would own and enjoy it for a long time. And, I paid market value for the car. He was a sharp owner and had done his homework on values.

When I handed him the check and he handed me the title, both of us felt good about the transaction. And, we remain friends to this day.

2
GENESIS
OF A BARN FIND
HUNTER

"Tom, you almost sideswiped that truck," my wife, the lovely Pat, scolded from the passenger seat.

"I know, babe, but did you see that Falcon in the field?" Just another day in the Cotter household where, by the way, my record stands at Thousands of Cars Spotted/Zero Wrecks (so far . . .).

But it started way before that . . .

I don't know exactly how old I was, perhaps nine- or ten-years-old. It was a different, safer time when parents let their kids roam the neighborhood on weekends—maybe even a few neighborhoods—as long as they were home and washed up by dinnertime. My friends and I were playing at Nokomis, the new elementary school in Holbrook, New York, where I was enrolled as a student.

A large housing development abuts the school now, but back then, it was just woods with an old dirt road running through. At some point when we tired of the playground, we explored that dirt road, which had its share of trash and abandoned refrigerators, farm implements, and cars. I remember spotting an old Roadster body, either a Model A or '32 Ford, with no frame, no fenders, no drivetrain, just the bare body. I can remember to this day the chrome handles next to the rumble-seat trunk lid. The car was painted black.

It reminded me of the hot rods I had seen on TV and in magazines. Standing there in the woods, I began to formulate a plan: I could build a chassis out of 2 x 4 boards like my father had around the house. Maybe I could use two skinny bicycle wheels in the front and snow tires in the back.

I called my friend Ricky Anderson over to look at the body and revealed my plan. "Want to drag it home with me and help me build it?" I asked.

"No way," he said. "You're not going to get me involved in that," a reference to another automotive misadventure I had recently engaged him in that never materialized as promised.

Unable to drag it home myself, that was that. I could have been the world's youngest Highboy Roadster owner, but I probably ran back to the school to play baseball or something. And sadly, that body was crushed by bulldozers when they cleared the land for houses.

As an East Coast kid, I devoured *Hot Rod* and *Rod & Custom* magazines, hoping to somehow live the West Coast hot rodder lifestyle. To this day, nothing gets my blood pumping more than when I see a classic Deuce roadster. *Tom Cotter Collection*

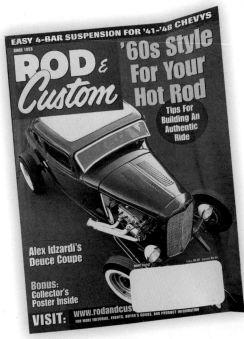

EASY 4-BAR SUSPENSION FOR '41–'48 CHEVYS

SINCE 1953

ROD & Custom

'60s Style For Your Hot Rod

Tips For Building An Authentic Ride

Alex Idzardi's Deuce Coupe

Bonus: Collector's Poster Inside

VISIT: www.rodandcus... FOR MORE EDITORIAL, EVENTS, BUYER'S GUIDES, AND PRODUCT INFORMATION

The first old car I owned, actually my brother Rob and I owned it together, was a late 1950s/early 1960s Fiat 1100 sedan. I was about twelve-years-old and my family was driving to McArthur Airport (now known as Islip) on Long Island. It was a Sunday afternoon, and we were on our way to pick up my grandmother who was flying in from Boston for a visit. On the way to the airport, driving down one of the back roads behind the runways, we saw a small car that had obviously been abandoned on a dead-end road.

"Dad, Dad! Can we stop?"

We couldn't stop because we were already late to pick up Granny. When we arrived at the terminal, we discovered that her flight would be delayed by a couple of hours, so on the way back home, we stopped to look at the little car. It turned out to be a Fiat in very sound condition, probably because it was only a couple of years old. Opening the hood we found that the cylinder head had been removed, suggesting an engine rebuild gone bad. Out of frustration or lack of talent or money, the owner seemingly towed it to the dead-end road and called it a day.

"Dad, Dad! Can we bring it home?"

Since we had some time before Granny's flight and home was only a few miles away, our father agreed. We went home to get a rope, returned, and tied the Fiat to the back bumper of my mother's VW Beetle. My father drove the VW, and I steered and operated the brakes in the Fiat. This was a life-changing moment for me, marking the first time I had ever "driven" a car. We made it home without drama, pushed the car in the backyard, and went back to fetch Granny.

In the days and weeks that followed, Rob and I "modified" our new car making it resemble a Monte Carlo or African Safari rally car like the ones we'd seen in magazines. We mounted the spare tire on the roof, added rally stripes, and put numbers on the doors using electrical tape. When friends came over, we'd take turns pushing and "driving" the car around the backyard of our quarter-acre plot. High speeds eluded us.

Eventually, my mom convinced my dad that we needed to junk the car, for what reason I don't remember, because it was good, clean fun that prevented us from otherwise developing bank-robbing or money-laundering skills. My father visited Louie Longo, a man who lived in the woods behind our house and had his own home-grown junkyard. My father arranged for Longo to tow the Fiat into the enveloping woods that surrounded his junkyard. My father and brothers Rob and Peter climbed in and I took the wheel for the Fiat's last ride.

The Fiat exited my life more than half a century ago, but I still think about it, and Rob and I occasionally reminisce about what we "should" have done with it.

I wonder if it's still resting in the forest behind my boyhood home?

The monthly column "Vintage Tin" exposed me to the concept of "finding" old cars and the possibility of buying them at below market value. It led to my purchase of a 1940 Ford convertible for twenty-five dollars. The cars those darn West Coast guys bought had little or no rust; not something we were used to on the Atlantic side of the continent. *Tom Cotter Collection*

When I was young, there was something about hot rods that made them so special to me. I collected cards called Hot Rod trading cards, which featured mainly cars that belonged to members of the Los Angeles Roadsters Car Club: Deuce Roadsters, Model As, '34 Fords, and '40 Ford coupes, sometimes appearing solo, sometimes gathered in a driveway or a parking lot in a club setting. There was something about the bright Candy Apple colors, the wheels, and the engines that made this East-Coast kid wish he had been born about 3,000 miles west.

On Sundays, my mother dropped me off for 9 a.m. Mass at St. Joseph's Catholic Church in Lake Ronkonkoma. After Mass, I would walk the five miles home, stopping along the way at Tom's Stationary to see if the new *Hot Rod* or *Rod & Custom* magazine had arrived. They were seventy-five cents, as I recall. Each issue was filled with cars like those on my Hot Rod trading cards, perhaps because Petersen Publishing issued those magazines and the cards as well.

Exiting Tom's Stationary, I would walk the remaining four miles home while reading the magazine. By the time I was home, I had it read.

The column I enjoyed the most was "Vintage Tin," which featured cars that readers had found in junkyards, barns, farm fields, and backyards. They were mostly old Fords—'32 Roadsters, '40 coupes, Ford T-Buckets—with surface rust because they had languished in a desert for years. These were project cars waiting to be made into hot rods by their new owners.

I suspected that most of the "Vintage Tin" cars featured in *Rod & Custom* had been discovered in California. Damn those California guys! They had hot rods, surfing, blondes, Coors Beer, and "Vintage Tin." And I was stuck in New York.

MEETING YOUR
HEROES

Tommy Ivo's Buick-powered T-Bucket was his daily driver, show car, and drag racer. Of all the iconic cars he has built in his life, this is the one he most regrets selling. *Tommy Ivo*

From my adolescent-gearhead viewpoint, there was no more prototypical California car guy than my automotive hero drag racer "TV" Tommy Ivo. He had a different look than the rest of the drag racers I saw in the magazines: clean white t-shirts, neatly combed blonde hair, and always a big smile. He was a drag racer even your mother could love. Years later, as an adult, I had the good fortune to write Tommy's biography.

"TV" Tommy Ivo: Drag Racing's Master Showman details his life and each of the cars he drag raced. One of the first cars he built was a 1923 Ford T-Bucket in 1956. Powered by a Buick nail-head V-8, it was one of the first T-Buckets built and resembled Norm Grabowski's similar Cadillac-powered *Kookie* Car.

When I interviewed Tommy, I asked him where he acquired the T-Bucket's body. Since fiberglass Model T bodies were still decades in the future, where did his metal bucket body come from?

"In those days, 1956, you could actually drive out into the desert and look around for an abandoned Model T," he said. "So, some friends and I drove out to Palmdale, which is north of Burbank. We drove around and around and saw this old Model T touring car body that had a Yucca tree growing right through the middle of it. That's probably why it was still there, plus it was just way too far off the highway."

Ivo had to drive back home to Burbank to pick up a handsaw so he could cut down the tree.

This would be a great *Barn Find Hunter* episode, but actually took place more than six decades ago!

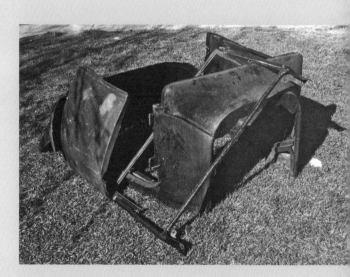

From this pile of parts, mighty hot rods do grow . . . Actor and drag racer Tommy Ivo found the remains of this 1923 Ford Touring Car sitting in the desert with a Yucca tree growing through it. After he cut down the tree, he brought it home and built one of the most influential T-Buckets in history. *Tommy Ivo*

DATSUN 510

It was 1978, and though I wasn't out searching for cars, I happened to stumble across one. That car has been in and out and in my life ever since. At that time, I owned a repair shop called Sunshine Garage in Blue Point, Long Island, that specialized in Japanese cars. I don't remember precisely why I was heading west from Blue Point on Sunrise Highway that day, but it was likely to chase down a much-needed part for a customer car.

My business partner John McDonald and I worked hard and did good work but sadly made very little money. We rented a small, unheated, rat-inhabited shop south of Sunrise Highway. Replacing clutches and performing valve jobs in the winter often meant enduring single-digit temperatures. It was frequently warmer outside, standing in the snow, than working indoors because at least the sun raised the temperature around us.

Anyway, I was driving my semi-wrecked Datsun 620 pickup down Sunrise Highway when I saw a Datsun 510 sedan sitting forlornly next to a gas station. Of course, I had to stop. A couple of years earlier, I had worked for a foreign auto parts store wheeling their 510 two-door sedan to deliver orders. It was a competent little car if ever there was one: overhead-cam engine, four-wheel independent suspension, disc brakes, wrapped up in a tidy package that rivaled BMW and Alfa styling. When that delivery car blew its head gasket, which later learned was a common problem, the store sold it to me for one hundred dollars.

Towing home my newly purchased, $250, 1972 Datsun 510 behind my 1976 Datsun 620 pickup (that needed a left-front fender) in 1978. I autocrossed, time-trialed, rallied, and raced that car throughout the Northeast. I was inspired by Datsun 510 racers Pete Brock, Bob Sharp, and Paul Newman. *Tom Cotter*

I raced the Datsun for a few years, at tracks like Lime Rock, Pocono, Bryar, and Summit Point. Here is a photo of my car (right) after a hard-fought, race-long dual with my late friend, Mario Birardi, at my home track, Bridgehampton Race Circuit. Soon after this photo was taken, I sold the car to Mario when I moved to North Carolina to become involved in the professional auto racing industry. *Tom Cotter*

When I got the car back (for free!) twenty-six years later, it was in pretty rough shape. The only thing to do was to totally disassemble and restore it. My son and favorite co-restorer, Brian Cotter, and I tore it apart and began the long process of getting it back on the road and/or track. *Pat Cotter*

As this book was being published, the Datsun had just been painted and was waiting for me to give it some love. I intend to build the car into the one I couldn't afford to build in the late 1970s. *Tom Cotter*

I installed cool wheels, a RACEMARK steering wheel, Interpart springs and shocks, and painted it a mild shade of yellow. But I was racing against time: the tin worm had infected the car and no matter what rust repairs I made, it was a lost cause. I wanted to road race a 510, but clearly mine was not the one.

So, when I saw that fairly clean two-door sedan next to the gas station, I pulled right in. As I walked toward the car—painted in the color I have since referred to as "Baby Shit Brown"— I saw that it had been lowered and wore Cosmic wheels. It had also been hit in the rear and would certainly need a new taillight panel. The guy inside the station told me it belonged to a customer, and yes, it was for sale: $250.

Long story short, I bought the car, had the rear panel replaced, installed a rollbar, rebuilt the engine, and raced it at tracks like Bridgehampton, Lime Rock, Bryar Motorsports Park, Pocono Raceway, and The Summit Point Circuit for a couple of years before moving south to pursue a career in motorsports. I sold the car to fellow 510 enthusiast Mario Birardi.

But that's not the end of the story. In fact, it's not even the barn find part of the story. That would happen twenty-six years later.

One day my phone rang, and the caller identified himself as Ronnie. He asked me if I used to race a mustard-colored Datsun 510. "Well, yes, actually more Baby Shit Brown," I said. "About a quarter-century ago."

"Well, I have it in my backyard, and you can have it for free if you want it."

I was on the case! How could I have imagined that when I sold my car while living on Long Island, that twenty-six years later it would be sitting in a backyard in North Carolina, about one hour from my house?

The car was rough, having sat outside for many years. Still, I had to take it. My friend Keith Irwin welded in another new back taillight panel and patched some rust in the quarter-panels. Surprisingly, the floors were still solid, no doubt the result of the gray deck paint I had brushed on when it became a race car (all race cars have gray interiors, don't they?).

I have collected a bunch of parts—a built 1800 cc engine, five-speed gearbox, new taillights— and recently retrieved the car from Keith's spray booth. It looks great. I debated whether to paint it Baby Shit Brown again, but decided I liked a medium blue, late-1950s VW/Porsche color.

What goes around comes around . . .

Inspired by the hot rods I was reading about, I was certain I could build one if I just had the chance; and the parts; and the tools; and the skill; and the money; and a garage. So at fourteen, as my friends played baseball or pursued the opposite sex, I collected Model A cabriolet components: a body with a chopped windshield, a bare chassis, a dashboard, and a few other parts.

An older kid, probably seventeen, named John Heaton, lived on Avenue B (I lived on Avenue A) and told me he would sell his Model A for twenty-five dollars because he was building a 1955 Ford pickup drag car. So, I bought it and dragged it home, although I can't remember how because it did not have wheels or even a suspension.

Somewhere, I had also acquired an early Ford V-8 banjo rear-end conversion setup, something way too wide for the skinny Model A body and chassis. When I inquired with a machine shop about having the axles and housing narrowed, and they told me $200, I stopped dreaming about that project. I had zero money and couldn't pay those crazy high prices. In high school, I sold that car to a friend, Joe Clay, who had a garage and tools and a father and brothers who could help him. He was making good progress on the car until a brain aneurysm struck him down soon after graduation. He was the first car-guy friend I had lost. When I visit my old stomping grounds now, I often wonder if the old Model A might still be sitting in his parent's garage.

Absent a hot rod or girlfriend, I thought being a priest might be cool livelihood. At my urging, my parents enrolled me at Seton Hall High School, a private Catholic school located in Patchogue, New York, on the South Shore of Long Island. Cars and girls returned and quickly eliminated the priesthood as a career choice, but I enjoyed my two years there.

At a science fair my freshman year, I met a fellow student sporting a "Lotus" lapel pin on his blue blazer.

"Lotus, that's a race car, right?" I asked.

At this point in my car-guy evolution, I was more of a hot rod and drag racing enthusiast, so Lotus was only vaguely familiar to me.

"Yes, they build Grand Prix cars, race cars, and street cars," said Xavier "X" Lucena, fellow car enthusiast and immediately my new best friend. X was much more into *Sports Car Graphic* magazine than *Hot Rod*. But in small Seton Hall, car enthusiasts were rare, with most students more interested in golf or tennis. He explained that Jim Clark raced a Lotus in the Indianapolis 500 and that they dominated sport car racing.

After school, X and I would wander the streets of Patchogue, the Long Island town where Seton Hall was located, in our blue blazers and ties. If we spotted an old car in someone's backyard, we'd innocently knock on the door to ask if it was for sale. As if we had any money . . .

We were on the school's cross-country team and running through a neighborhood during a 5K workout when we saw an old car in the driveway of an equally old house. We peeled off from the rest of the team to knock on the door.

An old woman answered. No, the car was not for sale, she said. She explained that she had purchased the car, a 1931 Chevy sedan, brand new some forty years earlier and that it was the only car she had ever owned. She asked us to wait for a moment while she retrieved something for us from inside her house.

We were hoping for chocolate chip cookies or lemonade, but it was even better: a copy of *Hemmings Motor News*, which at the time was the size of *Reader's Digest*, but very thin. Neither of us had ever heard of *Hemmings* before.

"If you like old cars, perhaps you can find one in here for sale," she said. "When my car needs parts, *Hemmings* is where I find them."

This was an outcome contrary to what I envisioned and in some respects, provided some direction to my nascent car-guy life. *Hemmings* became something of a "club newsletter" for enthusiasts with similar automotive interests, and I still utilize it today, fifty years later.

Bless me, Father . . .

Still in junior high, I heard about a 1938 Ford sedan, sitting in the woods behind a house with the name "Sherbo" painted on the mailbox. Sure enough, I walked through the forest behind the house and there rested the untouched Ford, seemingly driven there and parked on what was likely the back lawn before the woods took root.

I knocked on the Sherbo's door and asked if the car might be for sale. "No."

Still, I didn't feel good about leaving the car to disintegrate in the woods. I wanted to remove parts and either use them on my own projects or sell them.

Being a good Catholic-school student, I turned to Father Suave with my dilemma. The car was literally rotting in the woods, I explained, would God view it as a mortal sin if I removed parts from it?

"If the car is deteriorating because the people don't care for it, you can remove the parts and God won't think any less of you," he reasoned.

Hot dog! A holy Get-Out-of-Jail Free card! My friends and I removed a bunch of parts in short order, because, well, God said it was okay. I came to realize later that stealing is stealing, even if you have semi-approval from the church . . .

Feature Car of the Month

1916 Ford owned by Charles MacKinion, Jr., Newburyport, Mass.

New Rates For First Class Mail Are $4 Yearly, Airmail $6.50 Yearly. (See article on next page)

I was introduced to *Hemmings Motor News* at thirteen-years-old by an old woman who owned a 1931 Chevy. Little did I realize it would still be my bible a half-century later.
Tom Cotter

I was seriously into what we would later call "barn finds" by the time I was in high school. I left Seton Hall High School after my sophomore year because my parents could no longer afford the $400 annual tuition, and I finished school at Sachem High School in the Sachem Central School District. Because this was a public school, with an actual Auto Shop class, I quickly made friends with other car enthusiasts. Not surprisingly, Auto Shop was the only class in which I ever achieved an A+ grade! And because I already owned the '39 Woody, I was quickly accepted by the greaser gearhead crowd.

I found a 1941 Ford Woody a few miles from home for seventy-five dollars. The wood was poor, but I talked my longtime friend Tommy Allen into buying it. Sadly, he did what many of us did when we were young and penniless: dream how cool it would be to drive it, take it totally apart, lose the pieces, and lose interest. I don't remember what happened with that car.

My friend Phil Braddock, with his big, bold Boston accent, declared he could separate old cars into two categories: "Squares" and "Rounds." By this, he called the early cars—Model Ts and As, Squares because their boxy roofline resembled a box. Rounds, were later model old cars, such as 1940s coupes and sedans, that had curved rooflines.

Once we cut school and drove to eastern Long Island to search for old cars. We were on Highway 25A, somewhere east of Riverhead, probably in Mattituck, when Phil hollered, "Pull over, I saw a Square!" Unlike today, the area was rural and agricultural. We pulled the car over and walked through trees and shrubs to locate the Square. Actually, it wasn't a Square at all, or even a car, but an outhouse! No wonder this Square was well off the road and partially hidden by vegetation. Still, we all got a good laugh and from that point yelled "Square" anytime we saw an outhouse.

When I was a senior at Sachem, I met Gary Hall, a fellow senior recently graduated from my former alma mater, Seton Hall. I met him in the most authentic, barn find way: I knocked on the door of his family's home and asked about the old VW Beetle sitting in the driveway. My love of VWs was in high gear, so I slammed on the brakes every time I saw one.

As it turned out, Gary was also a hunter of old cars, especially VWs, and the two of us searched the length and breadth of Long Island over the next several years. We remained friends for a long time and he was my Best Man when Pat and I were married.

Gary and I also had a term for old cars: we called them Sheds. Why? Because so many we found in people's yards and driveways had assumed new lives as storage sheds. They might be jammed full of car parts, lumber, dog food, you name it.

During this time, my mother worked at Brookhaven National Laboratory (BNL), located on the former U.S. Army base Camp Upton on Long Island. BNL was 5,300 acres and in many ways, functioned as its own town, featuring housing, stores, and recreational facilities located on site—it even had its own zip code! Many of the scientists working there had studied applied physics and were clearly operating on a different level than me. But quite a few of them drove, repaired, and raced sports cars.

One of the scientists offered me a Porsche Speedster for free. This would have been in the early 1970s. Gary and I drove out to BNL to check it out. It was complete except for an engine. But it was badly rusted and sagged significantly in the middle. We couldn't even open the doors for fear that the car would collapse in half.

I turned it down because the VW Beetles I was dragging home were in much better condition than this Porsche. Plus, it was so small and roofless, it wouldn't even qualify as a good shed . . .

Today, even that horribly deteriorated Speedster would likely sell for $50,000 to $100,000. If only I'd known.

Early in my old car life, probably 1968, before I even had a driver's license, I heard from a friend's cousin of an "old car island" off the coast of Rhode Island. I convinced an older friend, Jim Mooney, that we should make a trip there, a jaunt of about four hours from Long Island. Jim drove us in his Checker sedan to Bristol where we hopped the ferry to Prudence Island.

There was really no town on the island, just a small building which contained a store, Justice of the Peace, and Sheriff's office—all run by one woman. We walked in and asked about the old cars. She told us we could walk there, a field about a mile away. Jim and I started to walk there when a man—IN A 1940 FORD WOODY—pulled up next to us and asked if we needed a ride. As we climbed in, we told him we were old car enthusiasts and were looking for the field with old cars.

"I'll be glad to take you there," the man said. He told us how the field came to be filled with cars. "It's too expensive and complicated to put broken cars on a ferry boat to bring them back to the mainland, so for decades we've just parking them in the field."

He also told us cars on the island did not need license plates or insurance, and the local kids got real-world driving experience by navigating the island's rural roads before they could legally apply for a driver's license. The Woody we were riding in actually had license plates from the 1950s, which I imagined was when the car arrived on the Island.

Before he dropped us off, he told us that if we needed any parts from the cars in the field, we could simply take them! "Feel free to take what you need," he said before he took off down the road.

The field contained hundreds of cars, many Fords and Chevys, but I do remember at least one really decent Chrysler Airstream parked in a barn-like structure. All the cars seemed to be complete with body, mechanical, and trim bits in place. For old car guys, this was like Disneyland! It was reminiscent of a land that time forgot—we had stumbled into an automotive time capsule.

We didn't have enough time or the proper tools, but that first trip led to several more, when we brought a child's wagon so we could haul our toolbox and parts from the ferry to the field and back again. We collected huge amounts of mechanical parts and trim, but because the Island was surrounded by salt water, most of the sheet metal body panels were too badly rusted to retrieve.

The grand prize from our many Prudence Island trips was the Columbia Two-Speed overdrive rear axle and controls I was able to grab for my 1940 Ford convertible. Jim and I discovered it when we dove into a 1940 Ford four-door sedan to escape a driving rainstorm. Jim said, "Look at those controls under the dash, I bet this car has a Columbia underneath." When the rain let up, I searched underneath the rear and sure enough, it had a Columbia, which was a rare, desirable, and expensive option.

I never did install it, eventually selling the convertible and the rear-end separately. But what a desirable item, and it was free!

I haven't been back to Prudence Island since about 1972, when some high school car-guy friends and I made the trip. It was a much different place even five years later. Many of the cars had been further stripped, likely by other old car scroungers like me. I wonder if anything still exists there today? It may be time for a return engagement, although with the spike in scrap metal prices in the 1990s, I'm willing to bet those cars were crushed and sent to Japan, now likely a part of some Honda or Toyota. If any cars are remaining, I'm sure they are rusted beyond recognition.

THE CAR WAS LITERALLY ROTTING IN THE WOODS, I EXPLAINED, WOULD GOD VIEW IT AS A MORTAL SIN IF I REMOVED PARTS FROM IT?

BARN FIND HUNTER:
THE NEXT GENERATION

When my son Brian was just a little tike, probably four-years-old, he and I were riding around the North Carolina countryside one Sunday afternoon in our Porsche 356 coupe. At some point, I looked down at my fuel gauge and determined we'd better stop for gas soon.

We pulled in to gas up at a rural station. Brian surveyed the landscape from his car seat and noticed a rusty old Chevy truck, probably a 1949 or '50, partially stripped and sitting on cinder blocks off to the side.

When I got back in the car, Brian said, "Dad, why don't we buy that truck? We could fix it up."

That truck was beyond help, but Brian's comment meant more to me that you could imagine. Here was my very young son, and he got it! He had already bought into the idea of fixing up old cars. That was some twenty-five years ago, and we have never stopped working on old cars together, whether they were mine or his, street cars or race cars. Whenever we are together on holidays or vacations, we are always tinkering.

It's our favorite father-and-son activity.

My best friend, Brian, who also happens to be my son, has been helping me work on cars since he was about three-years-old. Lately, I have been returning the favor, helping him rebuild the engine in his Porsche 911 or race prepping his 1964 Mini Cooper. *Pat Cotter*

VIEW FROM THE
PASSENGER'S SEAT

by Brian Cotter, AMG Product Manager, Mercedes-Benz USA

Hunting for old cars has always been a part of my life thanks to my dad. When out for drives, he was always scanning the sides of the highway for junkyards, old barns, and fields, hoping to spot some hidden car. He seemed to know where every interesting car was located in the state of North Carolina. Sometimes, I would point out a car that I had spotted for the first time, and more often than not, my dad would know not only the owner, but also what other cars were on the property, in the garage, or the surrounding area.

Growing up, I was lucky to share in the excitement that my dad felt when he found one particularly incredible barn find: a 1967 Shelby GT500 stashed in a small carport. I remember riding along to look over the Mustang and then, a few weeks later, helping him load the car on a trailer to bring it home. My dad was thrilled with the Mustang, and so was I. But I was even more thrilled to take home a barn find Rupp minibike that had been parked next to that rare Shelby for just fifty bucks!

Finding a low-mile, completely original GT500 is an ultimate bucket list barn find for many people. While I am sure my dad loves finding cars like this due to their rarity, I get the impression that sometimes the most satisfying cars for him are those that are the most challenging to spot, despite many times being a more pedestrian vehicle.

"Look behind the house at the end of the road, up the hill . . . right . . . now!" my dad said, excitedly. "There's a Datsun 510 behind the house!"

For half of a second, probably less, the front fender of a 510 could be spotted, a quarter of a mile off the road, obscured by tall grass, a hill, and a house. He now owns this 510, which was full of bees when he towed it home.

Another particularly memorable hidden car that my dad spotted was a crew-cab VW pickup truck that he had previously owned.

"You can see the top of the roof if you look over the fence at just the right time," he told me.

Even knowing where *and* when to look, the faded-red VW was camouflaged by leaves and years of neglect. How he was able to see the car, identify what it was, and determine it was the *exact* VW that he previously owned is beyond me.

With all the great father-son adventures we've enjoyed over the years, the barn finding gene has rubbed off on me. Now, when I go for weekend drives or when I go for my daily jog, I keep my eyes peeled for interesting cars in garages, carports, and yards. I may never find something as desirable and rewarding as a Shelby GT500, but for now, the hunting process is reward enough. The excitement I feel when I can make out the silhouette of a long-forgotten car when I'm least expecting it keeps me hunting for more.

If there's anything I've learned from my dad's experiences, it's that you never know what you're going to find—a random garage could hold a Festiva or a Ferrari, a Scirocco or a Shelby. As my dad always reminds me, "They're still out there!" And as long as they are, I know he'll be hunting for them.

The 1939 Ford Woody I drive on the *Barn Find Hunter* series was actually a barn find that I discovered and bought in 1969 when I was fifteen-years-old. I found it on a Saturday afternoon sometime that spring. Previously, you met my high school car-guy friend Xavier. X and I were walking across a schoolyard that afternoon, probably en route to hunt old cars in his hometown of Brentwood on Long Island. As we crossed the baseball diamond, I looked into the backyard of one of the houses that bordered the schoolyard and couldn't believe my eyes.

"Look, X, a Woody!" I yelled. We ran over to the fence that bordered the schoolyard and gawked at the car from a distance. Because I was such a car nerd, I instantly knew the car sitting next to a barn was a 1939 Ford.

We ran around the fence to Wick's Road, turned left, and walked to where the Woody sat next to the barn. From the street, this car was not visible, so if we had not walked through that schoolyard, that Woody would not be in my garage right now. (Note: To find old cars, get off the beaten path.)

I knocked on the door of the adjoining house and a nice woman, Mrs. Taylor, answered the door.

"Hello, my name is Tom Cotter. We were walking through the schoolyard behind your house and saw that Woody," I said. "Might it be for sale?"

"Why, yes it is," said Mrs. Taylor. "It belongs to my son, Richie, who's a surfer. He had used the Woody for a couple of years to go surfing at Gilgo Beach, but he just bought an old bread van, and he can sleep and change into his wetsuit in that. He wants to sell the Woody for $300."

She gave us permission to go into her backyard and look at the car.

It was so cool and resembled the cars I had seen in *Rod & Custom's* "Vintage Tin" columns. The fenders were painted a muddy shade of brown, it had pretty good wood, and a Schaefer Beer tap handle served as shift knob on the floor shift. It was everything I had dreamed of . . . I wanted to be a hot rodder and a surfer, so this car fit the bill.

Upon leaving, I told Mrs. Taylor I would hopefully be back later with my father.

X's parents were strict and would not allow him to own a car before he was sixteen-years-old and had a driver's license. My parents, though, were a bit looser, and the ice had already been broken by my ownership of the 1940 Ford convertible. X and I decided I had a better chance of buying the car— except for that part where I had no money.

That night my dad and I returned to look at the car. Even though he was not a car guy, my father appreciated my enthusiasm for a car of his generation. We talked about how we could work on it together and both of us got excited. But then there was the bad news:

"We don't have $300 to loan you for it," he said.

Dammit. How could I borrow money from someone and not let this get away?

I made the classic novice restorer's mistake when I brought home the Woody: Instead of installing a new fuel pump and regularly driving my new purchase, I tore it apart with the intention of restoring it, despite having no money, tools, garage, or money! I eventually sold it as a "project" to a collector in Puerto Rico. *Tom Cotter*

I decided to approach Laura Dale. Ms. Dale was an older single woman whom I had worked for on weekends, washing her car, mowing her lawn, and working around the yard. She offered to loan me the $300, and I could work off the debt over the summer.

The Woody was mine!

I remember how exciting it was when we picked it up the following Saturday. The entire Taylor family was there, including Richie the surfer. His father, Mr. Taylor, owned a local lumber yard and proudly told us they had recently replaced the door panels with mahogany plywood.

Richie was a cool dude with long, blonde hair and an amazing blonde girlfriend. He was West Coast on the East Coast.

We tied the Woody with a rope to the back of my mother's new VW Squareback, me in the Woody, and began the twenty-mile trip home down the Long Island Expressway. I'm not sure if it was legal, but we made it home.

From that point, my dad and I made all the classic novice mistakes. The car needed only a fuel pump to be a road worthy vehicle, but because I was a year away from my driver's license, I figured I could restore the car in that time. Never mind that we had no garage, no tools, no money, and no experience; we totally disassembled the car. My dad invested a couple of years of weekends refinishing the wood body, only to have it all come undone each winter as it sat under a heavy piece of damp canvas.

I eventually became more interested in hanging out at the beach with my friends, and by this time, I already had a girlfriend, my future wife Pat. My dad fiddled with the Woody when he could, but in 1973, I decided to sell it to pay for college.

It was about thirty percent restored at the time I sold it to Ernesto Rodriguez from Puerto Rico, a collector who rented his old cars for television and movie sets. He gave me $1,250, and I said goodbye to Woody forever . . . or at least twenty-six years.

Pat, now my wife, located the car via the National Woody Club, still in Puerto Rico. After befriending the car's then owner, Ted Lopez of Ponce, a couple of years later, I was able to buy it back.

And now, twenty-three years after re-acquiring my 1939 Woody, it has a new life as my co-star on *Barn Find Hunter*.

After I had completed restoring the Woody with a new modern drivetrain, I drove it 700 miles from North Carolina back to Long Island to show it to Richie Taylor, the guy I had bought it from those many decades ago. He had not aged as well as the Woody. His remaining blonde hair had gone gray. He had married his surfer girlfriend. She became a doctor and he continued to surf. The marriage didn't last. Richie inherited his parent's house when they passed, but he had let the beautiful homestead become a hovel. And he could barely walk, the result, if I remember, of a broken back.

Still, seeing his old Woody, all fixed up that day, brought a bit of sunshine into his life.

(TOP) When my wife, Pat, discovered the car twenty-six years later, still in Puerto Rico, we purchased it back. In the intervening years, the original wooden body was discarded and a new "cabinet style" body was constructed of teak. It was interesting, but I decided to have a new original style maple and ash body constructed. *Tom Cotter*

(LEFT) The finished product has serviced me well over the past few decades. The Woody has been a reliable companion in several cross-country trips and has been my companion in the YouTube video series *Barn Find Hunter. Tom Cotter*

Starting barn find hunting so early in life taught me some amazing lessons on how to negotiate the purchase of a car. But it also taught me one difficult and frustrating lesson:

SOMETIMES A "NO" ANSWER TRULY MEANS NO, ESPECIALLY WHEN CONFRONTING THE DREADED HOARDER.

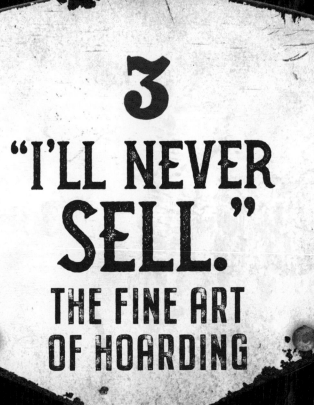

3

"I'LL NEVER SELL."

THE FINE ART OF HOARDING

"THE DIFFERENCE BETWEEN A HOARDER AND A COLLECTOR IS THE ILLUSION OF ORGANIZATION."

Mitch Silver, Silver Auctions, as told to Keith Martin

I've heard it at least a thousand times during my barn finding career. I'll be driving down the road and spot a dull, metallic object out of the corner of my eye as I pass. It's a car, the brand and year make no difference.

I'll drive up the road, wondering if I should turn around and inquire about it. Usually, within a mile or so, I'm searching for a driveway or parking lot in order to safely make a U-turn and head back to take closer look.

The car is sitting behind the garage, only partially hidden from the road, an easy mark for the probing eyes of passing car guys.

I won't be the first person to inquire about the car, nor, likely, the last.

The owner, whether a man or a woman, is usually kind and will to talk about the car, but eventually comes to the point:

"I'll never sell. I'm going to fix it one day."

If you've ever knocked on the door of that house, I'm willing to bet you've heard it too.

What is it that prevents people from selling the abused and neglected car to someone who will refurbish, appreciate, and enjoy it? I have several theories:

1. "It's my ball, and I'm going home." In other words, I own this old car, you don't, and I can do whatever the hell I want with it. Car folks with this attitude probably have a similar attitude about many things in their life. They are probably not charitable to those less fortunate, they probably don't pick up litter on the sidewalk, and they likely wouldn't help a little old lady cross the street. They would rather a car in their possession rust into the ground than let someone else enjoy or profit from their vehicle. I suspect they either grew up as an only child and never learned to share or in a large family with lots of kids where siblings often took possession of their private things.

In my wild imagination, I view the owner like this: He was a greaser in high school. He wasn't the all-star quarterback, and he didn't have a cheerleader as a girlfriend. He was a social outcast who worked in a gas station and on his hot rod after school and weekends. There was nothing interesting about this guy. Except that now, fifty years later, the quarterback is 300 pounds, has a bad back, drinks too much, and his cheerleader wife has long since divorced him. Our greaser, on the other hand, still has his high school set of wheels. Suddenly, he's pretty popular because he has owned that car for decades, and everybody wants to buy it. Now, he's the main attraction.

(RIGHT) Remember that greaser in high school, the guy with dirty fingernails and low grades? He had the fastest car in the school parking lot. (BTW, I resemble that remark.) Now, a half-century later, his old muscle car attracts enthusiasts to his door, and suddenly, he's popular!
Michael Alan Ross

(OPPOSITE) The saddest discoveries are those where the long-time owner intended to "park" the car for a short period while a part was sourced or a small repair was performed, only to have the car deteriorate after decades of exposure to the environment.
Jordan Lewis

For Mr. Greaser, to sell that car would be losing the most interesting thing about him, part of his identity.

You'll read in an upcoming chapter about the famous singer of the 1930s to 1950s, James Melton. Melton was quite a car collector and actually published a book in 1954 titled *Bright Wheels Rolling*, which in part describes how he obtained his cars. One specific car he desired was a 1906 Rainier and he finally located one in Ohio. As Melton related in this book:

"It belonged to a man named Paul M. Howard. I went around to see the car a couple of times a year, trying to persuade Mr. Howard to sell it to me, but he wouldn't. Finally, he told me why. He said he enjoyed having me come around and he was sure that if he sold me the car I'd stop coming. So I promised him I'd come to see him anyway, car or no car. He let me have it then. That was in 1945. I went to visit him at least once a year from then to his death."

Some seventy-five years later, there is still a lesson there for all of us.

2. "I'm just about to start working on it." I want to scream! When I hear those words, I'm nodding and smiling, but inside I want to say, "You fool! Forty years ago you parked a perfectly good muscle car under the tree in your backyard fully intending to repair the brakes, replace the clutch, or whatever. And now that the floors are totally rotted, you're just about to start working on it?" Of course, I would never say that to an owner because all conversation would end at that point. But it just doesn't add up. Most cars I've seen in these circumstances are ready for the scrap heap because at one hundred dollars per hour labor rates, the owner would be financially upside down within the first few days of restoration.

The hardest cars to discover are those stored indoors. But when you find them, what a relief . . . sheltered and protected from the elements. God Bless the hoarder who has a large garage. *Jordan Lewis*

No matter how handy the long-time owner might be, restoring a car is serious business, consuming hundreds or thousands of hours and cubic dollars. In reality, restoring the car is beyond even the most well-intentioned owner, requiring talents they probably don't possess. That they'll miraculously restore the car one day is a little lie they keep telling themselves to justify their continuing ownership.

I realize that for many owners, parting with their car would be like giving up a piece of their past—owning that car allows them to recall happier times, and I am sympathetic to that. But I also know that retaining such a car can be a burden. When I've met folks who eventually sold their long-owned car, it was like a weight had been lifted, and a new phase of their life was about to begin.

Attachment to their old car lasts beyond ownership, so wise buyers keep the previous owner involved in the car's refurbishment and at the conclusion of the restoration, offer to take them for a drive or even let them drive it.

I reluctantly sell my cars, but Pat often makes a good point, "Tom, if you haven't driven or worked on that car in the past twenty years, what makes you think you will in the next twenty?" As much as I'd like to argue the point, she's right. So, I'll reluctantly put the car on the market, not knowing how I'll survive without it. But when it eventually sells, I rarely regret my decision. The car is out of my life and into someone else's. And that's not necessarily a bad thing.

For you, the hopeful next caretaker of a desirable car, it's better to begin a friendly dialogue with the owner and cross your fingers you will get a phone call before it gets much worse.

3. Hoarding. Some folks simply cannot part with items from their past. It can include cars, car parts, newspapers, shoes—really anything. The American Psychiatric Association explains it this way:

> People with hoarding disorder excessively save items that others may view as worthless. They have persistent difficulty getting rid of or parting with possessions, leading to clutter that disrupts their ability to use their living or work spaces.
>
> Hoarding is not the same as collecting. Collectors look for specific items, such as model cars or stamps, and may organize or display them. People with hoarding disorder often save random items and store them haphazardly. In most cases, they save items that they feel they may need in the future, are valuable, or have sentimental value. Some may also feel safer surrounded by the things they save.
>
> Hoarding disorder occurs in an estimated 2 to 6 percent of the population and often leads to substantial distress and problems functioning. Some research shows hoarding disorder is more common in males than females. It is also more common among older adults—three times as many adults 55 to 94 years are affected by hoarding disorder compared to adults 34 to 44 years old.

My experiences searching for old cars seems to square with the psychiatrist's explanation. So many "collectors"—more junk collectors than car collectors—whom I've met over the decades fall into that 55 to 94 age group. I could never understand why a person of advanced age kept buying cars just to park them next to all the other cars, mostly stored outside to further deteriorate. Many times, some disassembly was begun, with parts and hardware scattered about, making sale or reassembly difficult.

Janice Lee Moskowitz, MHC-LP (Mental Health Counselor, Licensed Psychologist)—whose father-in-law is a non-hoarding car collector friend of mine—further educated me on an ailment some of us may suffer from:

"If clutter prevents normal life, when there is barely any room to move around, that is hoarding. Hoarding is an obsessive-compulsive disorder where having more pieces helps complete a collection and it becomes endless. Hoarding happens gradually and is usually the result of a trauma. Hoarders often believe that their collecting will lead to perfection, but it becomes overwhelming."

When trying to wrest a car from a hoarder, happy endings are rare. Sometimes, that car of your dreams will remain just that: a dream.

Regardless of his or her reasons for not selling the car sitting in the garage or in the backyard, it's best to leave a good impression with the owner and stay in touch. Drop by once in a while, maybe leave off a gift or interesting item relating to the car and reinforcing your interest in it. But also start searching for another car. There are plenty of fish in the sea, as the old saying goes. Don't waste your life trying to squeeze water from a stone. Stay in touch, but move on, determined to find something even better.

Hoarding is not the only human derangement I've had to deal with in my barn find adventures. On a Route 66 trip when I was both writing a book and filming our first prototype episodes of *Barn Find Hunter*, we were driving through a rural section of Arizona just as the sun was setting. We passed a ramshackle house with a number of old cars scattered about: a 1960s Cadillac, a Ford Falcon, a couple of VWs, and a few other cars, as I remember. It was getting dark and cold, but we decided to make one more stop before calling it a day.

I walked up the house and knocked on the door as the video crew removed their gear from the van and began setting it up. It didn't appear that anyone was home, but eventually a rumpled man, about my age, came to the door.

"Who are those people? Are they with you?" he asked. "You're not from the government, are you?"

I tried to calm this guy's rattled nerves.

"Oh, no, I have a show about finding old cars and wanted to see if you would let us film the old cars on your property," I explained.

"Why? What are you going to do with the video? How do I know you're telling the truth?"

I had obviously knocked on the wrong door because I suddenly didn't want to be there.

"You know, I've got guns. Plenty of them," he said. "I got a pistol on me right now and lots more in the house."

He finally relented and said we could photograph his cars, but he didn't want to be in the video or any of the photos. He walked down the driveway with me and began to loosen up.

"They were my father's cars, but when he died, they became mine," he said.

He had no plans to fix or sell them. Everything was cool until he saw the remote microphone attached to the collar of my shirt.

"What's that microphone?!" he shouted. "You're with the government, aren't you?"

I decided it was time to leave before our host began showing me his firearms and displaying his shooting prowess. He watched as we packed the vans with the camera gear and prepared to leave.

This hoarder of Checker Taxi Cabs parked them in the desert and forgot about them. Whatever the reason to acquire them, they've been taken out of circulation for the rest of us to buy, restore, and enjoy. *Michael Alan Ross*

(continued on page 54)

MORRIS MINOR

It was 1989, and it was my first visit to California's Sears Point Raceway (now called Sonoma Raceway). I was the PR rep for the General Foods' Country Time Lemonade brand on the NASCAR Winston Cup circuit. The driver was Michael Waltrip, who piloted a Pontiac fielded by Bahari Racing.

I had been traveling to virtually every NASCAR race for a couple of years, but an oval track is an oval track. Short track, intermediate, or SuperSpeedway, let's face it: all the turns are left! I was a road racing fan, and Sears Point would be just the second road course to host a NASCAR cup race in the modern era. Watkins Glen International in New York had joined the Winston Cup ranks in 1986.

Being at this celebrated race circuit, plus being in California—land of In-And-Out Burgers—was a thrill for this guy. One thing I knew about Sears Point was that it was ringed by industrial parks mostly occupied by sports car racers and restoration shops. In other words, right up my alley.

I walked around for hours over the course of the weekend when I was not needed in my PR duties. I'd poke my head into a building, look around, occasionally walk in and introduce myself as a fellow car-geek, and ask if I could look around.

Eventually, I arrived at Huffaker Engineering (now Huffaker Motorsports) a shop I had heard much about, a storied builder of race cars. Over the decades, Huffaker had fielded cars in SCCA's Can-Am, Trans-Am, and Production classes and various International Motor Sports Association (IMSA) categories.

In recent years, Joe Huffaker, Sr., had turned the reins over to his son Joe, Jr., who has done a great job in operating the business.

I walked into the showroom and looked at all the cool parts and race cars on display, but true-to-form, I needed to look out back to see if there were any old projects that had been put out to pasture. Of course there were, in particular a Richard Petty-blue Morris Minor two-door. I had owned a Morris Minor on Long Island several years earlier and had grown to like the little British cars. I walked back inside and asked Joe, Jr., about the car.

Joe gave me the keys. "Take it for a ride," he said. "The owner wants $1,200 for it."

Fair price, I thought. So, I walked out back to take it for a drive. I first kneeled down to inspect the underside. Being an East Coast guy, I had looked at a number of Morris Minors that were terribly rusty. These cars do not have separate chassis but are instead a unibody design basically fabricated of bent tin. Since this was a West Coast car, it was very solid. I started the engine, which rumbled to life but running on only three of its four cylinders. I put it into gear and made a couple of laps of the NASCAR paddock area and racetrack service roads, making sure all my redneck NASCAR friends saw me. I noticed the car jumped out of third gear.

I went back, parked the car, and returned the keys back to Joe, Jr.

"What did you think of it," he asked?

"I'll think about it," I said.

"Make me an offer. I need to get rid of it."

"Okay, $900," I replied.

"SOLD!"

Yee-Haw! A race car it did become! Converted from what the Brits consider a "Nannymobile," the Morris holds its own against much racier competitors, as well as putting smiles on the faces of many spectators, many of whom have their own Morris Minor stories. *Tom Cotter Collection*

Now, without telling Pat, I had just bought a $900 car that I needed to have transported 2,000 miles back home. Luckily, I was able to negotiate with one of the NASCAR teams to haul the car back for just fifty dollars.

The car sat in my backyard for a year or two until I decided to make it into a race car. My then three-year-old son, Brian, and I stripped that car down and built it back as a pretty good little racer that we had lots of fun with for several years.

Now, long retired, it sits quietly in a warehouse, a barn find once again.

I NEEDED TO LOOK OUT BACK TO SEE IF THERE WERE ANY OLD PROJECTS THAT HAD BEEN PUT OUT TO PASTURE..

The only time I felt threatened during a barn find expedition was when we pulled into this fellow's yard off Route 66 in rural Arizona as the sun was setting. He had some interesting cars, but the moment he started spewing paranoid and anti-government language, I wish I wasn't there. Thankfully, we made it out without incident.
Jordan Lewis

Before departing, I had to present him with a Release Form, which allowed us to use his property in our videos.

"I ain't signing nothing," he said as he patted a lump inside his jacket, obviously his pistol.

Before we pulled away, he asked for my business card in case he wanted to get in touch with me. I nervously gave him one.

Now, like that final scene from the movie *Deliverance*, I worry every day that this guy is going to show up at my front door.

Lately, if we pass old cars as the sun is setting, we just keep on driving.

4

TOP 25
BARN FIND HUNTING
PRO TIPS

"I'll see you at dinner time, Honey," I would tell Pat. "I'll be back once I find a Ford earlier than 1940."

She was probably glad to get me out of her hair for the day, but for me, this was the equivalent of adult treasure hunting. I lived on suburban Long Island until the mid-1980s and occasionally would get on my bicycle and tell Pat that I was going to spend the day searching for old cars around our neighborhood and around our town of Bethpage in Nassau County. I did this to prove you don't need to travel to the far ends of the earth to discover old cars; sometimes, automotive treasures exist just a few blocks from where you live.

Going on a business trip to the coast? Use your free time to look around.

Going on vacation to the beach or the mountains? Rural areas are an amazing resource for hidden old cars.

Picking up a pizza for dinner? Take a different route than you usually take.

After a lifetime of searching for old cars, I employ methods that after all this time come naturally, almost organically, to me. I suppose it could be considered a sixth sense ("I see dead cars."). I get a feeling when I see certain backyards or neighborhoods. A garage with grass growing in front of the doors? I'm all over it. Closed industrial buildings and rusty metal fences? I'm peeking in windows and climbing trees to look over the top.

I felt it was important to finally write down and share some of the tricks of the trade I've utilized for so many years. Below are the twenty-five tips that I live by. There is no guarantee these methods will put a dusty "new" barn find car in your garage or even that you'll get past the front door, but these methods should be essential items in your barn finding bag of tricks as you attempt to get to second base with the owner of a car you're lusting after.

1. DRIVE SOMETHING COOL.

This method has been further reinforced over the past few years during the filming of the *Barn Find Hunter* video series.

IT HELPS TO DRIVE A COOL CAR WHEN YOU WANT TO BUY A COOL CAR!

If you've watched the *Barn Find Hunter* series on YouTube or read my books, you are likely familiar with the 1939 Ford Deluxe Woody that I drive on most episodes. As I related previously, I discovered this car in 1969—when I was fifteen-years-old—as it sat beside a barn on Long Island. That Woody is the "icebreaker" for me when I park it in the driveways of otherwise "don't bother me" old car owners.

Rolling up in an interesting old car suddenly makes me as interesting to a car owner as he is to me. At the very least, it leads to an extended conversation and occasionally a glass of iced tea!

2. YES, YOU CAN GO HOME AGAIN.

If you are a car guy or gal, chances are good that the old car seeds were planted when you were a kid. Think back . . . do you remember someone in your neighborhood or your town who was a car guy? Someone who restored Model Ts, built hot rods, or raced stock cars or sports cars? If so, there is a chance that person, or their relatives, still lives there. And maybe, just maybe, some remnants of that person's obsession still remain—and they likely know where interesting cars are resting. I've tried it many times, and it works.

Recalling my childhood, I remembered seeing a driveway full of odd and wonderful little sports cars as my bus passed a certain house every day after school. I remembered that the house was also a doctor's office. Decades later, I went back and knocked on the door. A woman answered.

"Excuse me," I said. "Does a car guy live here?"

"No, but a car *person* lives here," she said without missing a beat.

She explained that her late husband, a doctor and car collector, had died a few years earlier and that she still owned all his cars.

"I had been praying that someone might come along and help me dispose of his cars. I think God has brought you to my door."

How could I have predicted that I was the answer to her prayers? She gave me a tour of her basement, where some of cars were parked, and of an airplane hangar about twenty miles away, where even more cars were parked.

In hindsight, I should have purchased all of her cars, probably a dozen that included a couple of Porsches (including a 930 Turbo), a Vette, two Fiat 500s and a rotary-powered hovercraft. It seems the doc was also quite an inventor and fabricator. But at least I did buy one car: a rare 1961 Abarth Monomille, which her husband had purchased new.

On another occasion, I decided to drive past a home on Long Island that I used to bicycle past as a kid. I remember cars being worked on in the driveway, especially an early MG. When I returned decades later, I peeked inside the garage and alongside several Model T Fords, there was a British MG TC Racing Green. And, yes, Nancy Moore, the owner, would sell it. I didn't buy it, but included a story about it in my first barn find book *The Cobra in the Barn*. After reading the book, MG collector Tony Giordano contacted me, asked about the car, and bought it from Nancy. He then turned a tidy profit when he sold it to a collector in England.

3. WEEKENDS ARE A BARN FIND HUNTER'S BEST FRIEND.

Unless they are retired, most folks go to jobs during the week. So, Saturdays and Sundays are your best friend. Surprised? Weekends are a time when folks are home doing yard work and other home maintenance. That means garage and barn doors may be open when they are normally closed. Look carefully, especially toward the rear or sides of the garage because sometimes something interesting might be parked there.

During one of my bicycle-riding search-and-rescue missions, I passed an open garage door that showed a pile of clutter: bikes, snow sleds, and yard equipment. But I studied the pile and noticed a taillight poking out.

Weekends are the best time to go searching for cars that are normally hidden behind garage doors because folks are often working on yard and home projects. Cars like this Porsche Speedster are like a needle in the haystack, but they are still out there! *Jordan Lewis*

I identified it as a Jaguar taillight. I approached the owner, who was raking leaves, and asked if he had a Jaguar XK120 in the garage.

"You gotta be kidding me," he said. "You can actually see a car under that pile of crap?"

Yes, there was a Jag in there, which he had owned since college. He was not interested in selling, but I think I made his day. He certainly made mine! I heard that a few years later, probably when his kids were in college or out of the house, that he unearthed the car and got it mechanically restored.

4. BY CAR, PEDAL, OR FOOT.

Just because you are looking for a car doesn't mean you need to be driving a car. Driving a car requires that you look out for other cars and pedestrians, which diverts a barn find hunter's attention from the task at hand. Bicycling or even walking (or running) are great alternatives when looking into garages, especially when traveling through suburban developments. When walking or riding a bike, it is easy to stop and turn around to see what that metallic object was that caught your attention. And I've gotten wonderfully refreshing responses from homeowners when I come riding or running up to their front door, far different than if I had driven up in an SUV.

5. "TOM, WILL YOU LOOK WHERE YOU ARE GOING?"

How many times have I heard that over the past four and a half decades from my wife? When driving down the road, I do have a habit of looking over my shoulder as I pass buildings. Let's face it, driving on a road going in one direction is a completely different road than when driving in the other direction. So, when passing roads or warehouses or homes or shops, I'm looking behind me about twenty percent of the time. Not the safest thing to do, I know, but I do try to carefully look ahead before turning my head.

Don't try this at home; or at least, when your spouse is in the car.

It also gives credence to my next Pro Tip: When searching for old cars on dead-end roads, you must drive on the same road in the other direction.

6. DEAD END AND NO OUTLET ROADS ARE BEST.

Nobody likes to drive down dead-end roads. Let's face it, you don't get anywhere! When you reach the end, you often have to do a three-point turn or back into somebody's driveway as the owner stops raking leaves and carefully watches your every move. It's never fun. However, as Robert Frost said in his poem, *The Road Not Taken*:

> Two roads diverged in a wood, and I—
> I took the one less traveled by,
> And that has made all the difference.

Cars are usually parked with the best intentions by their owners. Often a hard-to-find part or a mechanical issue will have a simple repair span decades. I'm not suggesting to trespass on private property, but cars like this 1957 Chevy would be impossible to find without peeking in the window. *Jordan Lewis*

Will it make a difference? Perhaps. Understand that folks driving around looking for old cars are just as turned off making U-turns at the end of a dead-end street as everyone else. Why would anybody choose to drive down a dead-end road unless: 1) You or a friend lived there; 2) You are delivering the mail; or 3) You are lost. My guess is that Dead End and No Outlet roads probably see less than twenty-five percent of the traffic of a normal through-road. And, I bet that plenty of old cars exist on these roads in the yards of owners who don't get many "door knockers" coming down their quiet lanes.

7. CHECK OUT THE BACK ROW.

Car projects usually begin with much gusto and enthusiasm, but once the hard work and expense is realized, they are often move to the back burner. Acquiring a new old car is exciting, and owners jump on their new hulk with wrenches, screwdrivers, and energy. But remember this: turning bolts counterclockwise is "free" and "fun;" turning them clockwise is expensive. Why? Because when those bolts go back on, they are invariably attaching parts that were rechromed, repainted, remachined, or rebuilt in someway.

Sometimes that cost realization takes place after the first couple of invoices from a body shop, welding shop, machine shop, or upholstery shop. Those in-process cars are often pushed out to the back lot where they are left to deteriorate as the owner tries to regroup financially or tries to forget about the project altogether.

All too often, shops do not charge a monthly storage fee, so the stillborn project is taking up valuable real estate. This makes shop owners more than eager to rid themselves of stalled projects.

Then, there are shop employees. Experience has taught me that most mechanics are, or at least were, enthusiasts. So during the day, mechanics are working on customer cars, performing brake jobs, and tune-ups. But nights and weekends, they can often be found working on their own project cars. Sometimes, those projects go stale when they require more money than budgeted or other personal matters take priority. And, again, those cars are pushed toward the back row of the shop.

Check out the back rows of repair shops, car dealerships, body shops, and restoration shops. Forget all the shiny cars up front; the real treasures are covered in blue tarps and surface rust in the back.

8. IT'S A BALLOON! OR, AT LEAST A DRONE.

I once spoke to an old car enthusiast who certainly had an advantage "over" the rest of us. He was a blimp pilot. He explained that he flew one of the commercial blimps—MetLife, I recall—which was stored much of the year in the New York area. But annually, he flew it south to Florida for major sporting events like the DAYTONA 500 and The Super Bowl. He said the trip was carefully scheduled to ensure on-time arrival for the activities, such as planning for the potential of bad weather. But the return trip north was more leisurely.

"On the way home I just fly down real low, and I'm able to snoop behind barns and fences that are not visible from the road," he said. He told me farmers sometimes come out of their houses to see why this huge lighter-than-air craft is hovering over their acreage and scaring the cows. "If I'm low enough, sometimes I'm able to actually talk to the farmer and ask him about his cars."

Ballooning is not an option for most, but a couple hundred bucks will buy a good drone and provide a similar bird's-eye view. My Hagerty film crew often packs a drone when we film episodes, usually just to give an interesting overhead perspective of a field of cars or of my Woody driving down the road. Once, though, we considered using it to spy on cars parked on private property.

It was north of San Francisco, along one of the many tributaries that feed the San Francisco Bay Area. We were visiting an odd old junkyard filled with American and foreign cars stacked up along a creek. I can't imagine the EPA approving something like that in modern times, but obviously this place has been in business long before people cared about keeping the environment clean.

But it wasn't that junkyard we were so intrigued with. Instead, it was the salvage yard next-door which was closed to the public. Apparently, the owner's father used to store and buy cars from incoming or outgoing soldiers stationed at nearby military bases. I was told that over the course of decades, the family had built up quite a collection of unusual vehicles. The father was deceased, but his son stood guard over the family's collection in the backyard behind the fence.

A local told me that a six-wheel WWII Mercedes-Benz staff car had once sat behind the fence. When Mercedes-Benz Corporate found out about it, they sent a couple of representatives from Germany with an open check-book to buy it. I have no idea how much they paid, but the owner finally relented. The staff car was flown that same day on a transport plane from San Fransisco directly to Stuttgart, Germany, and now sits in the corporate collection.

When I contacted the owner and explained our *Barn Find Hunter* series, he was nice, but said we were not allowed to come on his property. No matter how I tried, he wouldn't budge.

Having heard about the Mercedes and that there were other interesting foreign cars and race cars, I was so eager to gain access to the property, I even offered to leave all of our camera gear in the Woody. No-go.

That's when I asked my crew, "Why don't we just fly the drone over his property?"

I was told that we could get in legal trouble, "Um, that's trespassing, Tom." Besides, the owner probably would have shot it down.

(OVERLEAF) Some use airplanes or hot air balloons, but today, anybody with a drone can search for old cars from the sky. During *Barn Find Hunter* shoots, we regularly utilize a drone, but only after we've received permission from the landowner. *Jordan Lewis*

1.5 MINIS

It was wintertime in North Carolina, and it was cold. But it certainly wasn't as cold as it was at my old stomping grounds on Long Island. It was probably twenty-five years ago when a long-time Long Island car guy friend called to give me a lead on a couple of barn finds in the town of Northport, on Long Island's North Shore.

"There's a Mini Cooper sedan in the garage and a Mini Countryman wagon sitting outside," he said. "The owner is moving, so the cars are free, but they must be moved quickly because his house is for sale."

Well, that was a no-brainer. Unfortunately, I was almost 700 miles south. Hmmmm . . .

My brother-in-law, John Vignona, "Viggy," worked for my PR agency, Cotter Group, driving a show car hauler, a truck and trailer that hauled display race cars that were exhibited at shopping centers, racetracks, and other public locations. Like me, Viggy was a Long Island native.

"Hey, Viggy, I know you don't have any appearances for a few weeks. How would you like to visit your Mom and friends on Long Island for a few days?" I asked.

"When do I leave?" was his response.

Viggy departed the next morning in a "dually" Chevy truck with a forty-eight-foot trailer to retrieve the two Minis. When he called from the house the next day, he told me the owner had already vacated, but the garage was unlocked, so both cars were available.

Working alone, Viggy tried to push the sedan out of the garage and onto the snowy driveway,

When a friend offered me his 1964 1071 cc Mini Cooper, it was pretty rough, with actual rust holes on the roof. But a complete sandblasting and new metal fabrication turned it into quite a solid little car. Here is Brian pretending to race the car when he was about five-years-old.
Tom Cotter

but the tires were low on air, so it didn't move very easily. Thankfully, the trailer had a winch, so the Mini was rolled out of the garage and pulled into the trailer. Once that car was tied down, he moved to the station wagon. This car had issues even more challenging than the sedan. Because it had been stored outdoors for a long time, the tires had sunk into the turf. Compounding that was the fact that a layer of icy snow blanketed the frozen ground.

Viggy huffed, and he puffed, but he could not budge the small car. Luckily, the winch method had already worked once, so there was no reason to think it wouldn't work again. With the trailer repositioned, he hooked the cable up to the rear of the body and gave it a tug.

Nothing.

He gave it another tug. It began to move; then it stopped.

He pushed the winch button one more time, and the rear of the car moved while the front stayed frozen to the ground. The car had broken in half! This should come as no surprise to British car enthusiasts, as the cars are often unsafe rust buckets.

"Hello, Tom, I can only bring home the sedan," he said on a phone call.

I had already been planning to own two cars, so I was disappointed.

"How come?" I asked.

"The station wagon broke in half," Viggy said. "It's toast."

"Understood. Come on home."

The sedan turned out to be a great little car. I stripped it, had a roll cage welded in, and a new bright Mazda Miata–red paint job applied. The 1071 cc engine was rebuilt, and I both raced it and drove it on the street for years. The car had been sitting in my garage for a number of years, but recently, I gave it to my son, Brian. He intends to race it after a mild refurbishing.

Hopefully, my free Mini will give another Cotter generation additional years of fun! Although I do wonder what ever happened with that wagon . . .

Here's the same car, a few years and several dollars later. The car turned into a competent and competitive vintage race car, as well as the occasional street driver. Today, Brian owns and races the car. *Tom Cotter*

9. MAKE FRIENDS WITH POLICE OFFICERS, DELIVERYMEN, AND LANDSCAPERS.

You or I cannot walk onto private property without breaking the law and potentially getting bitten by a dog or shot! But some people generally have permission to step on private property legally. Those folks are UPS, FedEx, and postal delivery employees; landscapers, gardeners, painters, and other workers; and police officers. I regularly ask these folks if they know of anyone with old cars in their backyard, carport, or garage. An offer to give them a finder's fee, or a "bird dog" as we used to call it in the car business, if they can provide you a lead usually gets their attention.

One of three barn find Cobras I have discovered in my career—the brown CSX2149 that was featured in *The Cobra In The Barn*—was found in Indianapolis by a propane deliveryman who saw the covered sports car through a dirty window in a barn. He thought it was an MG or a Triumph, but it was actually the 149th AC 289 Cobra. At the time, it was the home of a raccoon.

I often ask police officers if they know of old cars. Some policemen are car enthusiasts, too, so when I asked a patrolman in Southport, North Carolina, he said, "Yeah, I know an old car. It's in my barn. Here's my address. I'm off tomorrow. Come over in the morning." The next morning, now dressed in car-guy blue jeans and a t-shirt, he proudly showed us the 1969 Chevelle he had owned since high school. The car had seen better days, but he said it "ran when parked" and he was looking forward to restoring it in the near future.

Parked for decades in an Indiana barn, this early Cobra provided lodging for a testy raccoon who had no intention of giving up his sporty digs. Eventually, my friend Jim Maxwell and I relocated "Rocky" and restored the car into a show winner.
Tom Cotter

I attended the California Hot Rod Reunion in Bakersfield, California, (an amazing tribute to drag racing history) where I struck up a conversation with a tree surgeon who told me he often has a great view behind fences and into backyards when plying his trade. So, add arborists to your information-source list.

---

* * * NEWS FLASH * * * THIS JUST IN * * * NEWS FLASH * * *

As I write this, I just got off the phone with a new friend, Larry Bauer, who lives on Kent Island, located in the Chesapeake Bay off Maryland. Bauer is a car guy with a passion for old VWs. He is also the owner of FIXD Garage Door Services. I am convinced that he has THE BEST JOB to find old cars: Bauer is called by wealthy people living on a secluded island to service their garage doors!

"I've been in the garage door business for about ten years, but I've been in my own business for three years," he said. "It's a tight-knit community, where everyone knows everybody else." So, most of his business comes from word-of-mouth recommendations.

His business consists of installing new doors, mostly for luxury home builders, repairing garage doors, adjusting springs, installing seals, and lubricating tracks. But think about this: Bauer is *invited* to come onto private property and into people's garages!

My new hero is Larry Bauer of Maryland, who owns a garage door repair company. He is invited by homeowners into their garages. He is often the first person in years to see long-time parked cars, which are frequently interesting and sometimes available for purchase. *Larry Bauer*

"I was hired to repair the doors on a garage at the end of a long drive-way," he said. "Outside were three Honda CRVs, no big deal. But when the owner opened the door, there was a Pantera with inches of dust, sitting on four flat tires. The owner told me he's owned it since he was in his 30s.

"These owners are usually super private, so I'm sure nobody knows cars like this are hiding in their garages."

Bauer told of one man who opened a garage that contained a collection of Ferraris. "He told me, 'Don't tell anybody!'"

"I learned that I must respect these people's privacy. But once I tell them I am also an enthusiast, they appreciate it, and they'll usually talk cars with me for twenty minutes."

He told me of one house that has a yard full of cars under covers, at least fifteen of them, that suggest Art Deco styling from the 1930s. Another house is surrounded by old Land Rovers.

"It's hit-or-miss," he says. "Every time I go to a new customer's home is another opportunity."

He notes the COVID-19 pandemic lockdown had people spending more money on their houses, and designer garage doors are something they are buying.

"One man, who is so private, has a Shelby R-Model Mustang, a GT350, a supercharged GT500, and an old Woody," said Bauer. "It seems that every town has five or six weirdo car people."

Bauer is also a bicycle collector and has an interesting story regarding a Schwinn Sting-Ray.

"I was over at a house to repair the garage doors and saw this black Sting-Ray bicycle sitting in the corner," he says. "It was in really good shape. I asked the owner about it, we talked a while, and I wound up doing the repairs in exchange for the bike.

"I had the bike for a while, but then found a 1988 Toyota 4Runner that the owner said needed lots of work. I've always liked these, and I was born in 1988. So, I traded the Sting-Ray plus $500 for the Toyota. It didn't need much work at all. I have it all fixed up, and it's on our family's Christmas card."

The moral of this story? Make friends with your local garage door repairmen.

---

* WE NOW RETURN YOU TO YOUR NORMALLY SCHEDULED BARN FIND TIPS *

---

10. CHECK OUT OLD CLASSIFIED ADS.

I have collected hundreds of old copies of *Hemmings Motor News*, *Road & Track*, and *Autoweek* with the sole intention of "one day" having the extra time to call the people who listed rare and unusual cars 10, 20, 30, or even 40 years ago.

My fantasy goes something like this: "Hello, this is Tom Cotter, and I was just scanning an old copy of *Road & Track*. I see that you were selling a 1967 Corvette with an L-88 427 engine in *Road & Track* magazine in 1980. I'm curious, maybe you didn't sell that car and maybe you still have it?"

I then agree to pay the seller the $5,000 he was asking for it forty years earlier. He's happy to finally clear that old car out of his garage, and I'm over the moon!

Then, I wake up . . .

Seriously, though, I guarantee there are still unsold and desirable cars that have been sitting for decades in lonely garages. If you have the time, give it a try. And let me know how you do.

11. WRITE LETTERS.

Let's say you have found an interesting old car you would like to own but the owner won't sell. Keep visiting and try to become the owner's friend. At some point, write a nice postcard or letter to the owner expressing your interest in the car should he or she ever change their mind.

Emails are easily deleted or lost in the ether, but physical mail is either thrown out immediately or gets "filed." Sometimes, those letters are stuck on the refrigerator; sometimes, they are filed in the desk, but I guarantee that mail seldom is thrown away. When the owner passes away or is moved into a nursing home, it's not unusual for family to sort through personal effects to put the estate in order.

Your letter presents an easy solution regarding that old car in the garage. Your note might lead to a phone call and maybe a purchase. Mopar collector Barry Lee of Jacksonville, Florida, found a Plymouth Superbird hidden inside a hedge that had grown around it, believe it or not. The elderly owner would not sell, so Barry's wife suggested they send a letter. "Call it woman's intuition, but she had a good idea," he said. Not long after the owner was moved to a nursing home, Barry received a call from the man's son-in-law, and he wound up owning that Superbird. Happy ending! Except he had to cut down the hedge to get it out!

12. WINTER IS YOUR FRIEND.

Don't get me wrong, summer is a beautiful time of year: the flowers are in bloom and the trees are full of leaves. But take it from this old barn finder: the best time to go hunting for old cars is in the winter. When leaves are on trees, your vision from the road is cut in half or worse. But in the winter, depending on what part of the country you live in, as The Who sang, you'll be able to "see for miles and miles and miles . . ."

Well, maybe not miles, but usually far enough to see shiny pieces of stainless steel or body panels. It's like having X-ray vision.

Of course, if you live in the southwestern United States, you don't have to wait until winter because your trees don't shed leaves. Plus, your cars are in much better condition. You guys have it made.

13. REVERSE PSYCHOLOGY.

If you see an early Ford Bronco or a Toyota FJ sitting behind the garage, congratulations. But trust me, you are not the first one to see it. And you're not going to be the first person to knock on the door and ask if you can buy it. I promise you, the owner has heard it all before. In no time, you'll be back in your car and on your way down the road.

But what if instead of asking about buying, you were offering to sell the owner something?

I've tried this and the results are interesting.

"Good morning," I'd say. "I see you have an old Bronco in the backyard." Then, just as the owner's eyes begin to glaze over, I ask, "Do you need any parts for it? My friends and I have a bunch of parts and know of others. I'd be glad to help you out." One caveat here: If the owner takes you up on your "offer" (nobody ever has in my case), you've got your work cut out for you!

Suddenly, in the owner's mind, you've gone from "just another door knocker," to someone who could be an ally. At the very least, this will give you a few more sentences with the owner before he closes the door in your face.

Use reverse psychology. Rather than asking if that Bronco (or fill in the blank) is for sale, instead, ask the owner if he might need parts in order to complete their restoration. It's an interesting idea that sometimes will get you to second base. *Jordan Lewis*

Another method when the owner says, "No, it's not for sale, I plan to restore it," is to offer to help him. Tell him (I'm using the pronoun "him," figuring a woman would make a better decision . . .) that you'd love to come over and help clean, organize, and take inventory of the project in an effort to make it easier when he actually begins the project. When I was trying to buy my Cunningham, I used a variation of this approach—asking if I could come over occasionally to photograph, research, and authenticate the car—which may have led to the owner to eventually telling me, "You certainly care more about this car than I do, I'm going to sell it to you."

No guarantees, but these are out-of-the-box approaches that sometimes work.

14. SIGNS OF THE TIMES.

I have owned HUNDREDS of cars in my life, and I'll bet that only a handful of those cars had For Sale signs posted when I purchased them. To me, once the owner writes For Sale across the windshield, it means they have done at least some research regarding its value.

With people trolling eBay or tuning to the Barrett-Jackson auctions, everyone thinks they have the most valuable car on the planet.

"Yeah, it's a rusty four-door Chevy Nova, but it's not just any rusty Nova. This one has the rare optional wire wheel covers," Jay Leno once jokingly told me.

But if you can inquire and potentially purchase an old car *before* the owner thinks about selling it, you might just score a bargain.

15. OLD BUILDINGS ARE YOUR OTHER FRIEND.

I love the sight of an old metal building, especially if it has a healthy layer of surface rust. Or, perhaps a cinderblock building that could have once been a commercial establishment but now has three-foot tall grass growing against the garage doors. Both these scenes tell me that some kind of industrial activity once took place there, possibly automotive, but that not much has happened in the recent past. This suggests that relics from the former business might remain inside. I often peak in windows at buildings like these and can report that cars are often stored inside.

Indoor cars are the BEST finds, especially if the roof of the building is watertight. But, no surprise, inside cars are the hardest to find for obvious reasons.

It's important to keep your eyes peeled for evidence outside, which might give clues to items inside the building: a fender leaning against a tree, a wire wheel used as a mailbox post, or an outside car lift or ramps that may reveal that the building was once used as a commercial repair shop. These clues give you "evidence" that cars may still exist on the property and present reasons to approach the owner.

LOOKING THROUGH
GARAGE DOORS

(Excerpted from Peter Egan's foreword to *The Cobra in the Barn*)

"A few years ago , I flew out to the San Francisco Bay Area, met Tom at the airport, and helped him drive his newly purchased, very original red 1964 289 Cobra across the United States, all the way back to his home in North Carolina. The trip took about a week, and we never even tried to put the top up. It was a good thing, too, because we later discovered the top had disintegrated in the trunk, from heat and old age.

I'm sorry the car did not come out of a barn—it lived in the neat three-car garage of its knowledgeable and sympathetic owner—but it hadn't been driven much in recent years and it needed a little roadside wrenching to make the trip. Nothing disastrous, mind you, just the stuff of good adventure.

The trip was filled with great memories, but my favorite moment came when we were cruising through a small town on the plains of eastern Colorado.

As we drove through the center of this little burg, Tom's head swirled back and forth like a radar dish, sweeping over the houses, fences, backyards, and buildings. He suddenly turned to me, grinning, with a strange, maniacal gleam in his eye.

'Don't you wish,' he said, 'that you had X-ray vision so you could spot all the neat old cars that are probably hidden away in these small town garages and old barns?'

Of course I did. I've had that very same thought a thousand times. We all have, even if we've never put it in words."

Behind closed doors are where the best finds hide. Short of X-ray vision, finding them requires guts (sneaking up to a window to peer inside), a lead from someone (maybe a friend of the owner), or simply knocking on the door and asking if there is something inside.

I suggest you look for "clues" that might be sitting outside the building. There is no correct way to do it: if your method works, it was correct; if it didn't work, you screwed up.

More barrier than building, rusty metal fences often hide vehicular relics as well. Junkyards, or folks with lots of junk, often buy cheap metal privacy fences or metal roofing to keep prying eyes from their "valuable" inventory. Or, perhaps the town or the county required the installation of a fence to hide the cars. I remember President Lyndon Baines Johnson's wife Lady Bird went on a tear to clean up the junkyards of America. Suddenly, all these salvage yards had metal fences installed and flowerbeds out front!

I've visited a few junkyards where old school buses actually served as fences to hide the junk inside. These are ideal fences because they both shield the junk inside and can be used as "storage sheds" themselves for transmissions, driveshafts, and other parts. Win-win!

My friend Kevin Mackay, a historic-Corvette race car guru, spent years searching for a rare Corvette, part of a three-car team, raced by Briggs Cunningham at Le Mans in 1960. He literally invested two decades searching for the car and had identified a neighborhood in Tampa, Florida, as the probable location. He flew from New York several times to knock on doors, trying to locate that car. He knew he was close, but he just couldn't find anybody who knew exactly where it was. Eventually, he hired a psychic to walk down alleys behind homes in a certain neighborhood to see if there were any "vibrations" he could detect from any of the garages.

The psychic never did locate the car, but it shows the lengths some hunters will go to in attempting to find a special old car.

16. "MAY I USE YOUR BARN FOR PHOTOGRAPHY?"
Classic barns and other old industrial buildings are often chosen by photographers as ideal backdrops for automotive photography. My friend Michael Alan Ross, a very creative and successful automotive photographer with whom I have collaborated with on five books, will search for days to find just the right background to highlight a classic, sports, or race car he is shooting.

If you see an interesting old building, asking permission to shoot photos there will not only yield cool photos of your car, it might also give you ample time to look inside.

If you are given permission, though, you had better have an above average car to photograph, and you had better have something better than a phone camera. Be prepared with a tripod and a "real" camera.

17. "IS THIS THE HOUSE WITH THE OLD CARS?"

A couple of car guys gave me this tip about three decades ago, and though I have never tried it, I'd say it sounds like a winning concept.

They told me that one Saturday morning they traveled to tony Newport, Rhode Island, from their homes nearby. They randomly selected one of the spectacular mansions along the ocean and knocked on the door.

"Excuse me, but we heard this is the house with the old cars," these guys said. "Can we please see them?"

They were told, no, they must be mistaken, that this was the wrong house. "But the man on the corner with the big white house collects old cars. Go see him."

They visited that neighbor, telling him the neighbor down the street recommended it; then, after seeing those cars and before departing, asked who else in the neighborhood had old cars. "Oh, go see the guy in the stone house; he has a garage full of old cars."

They did this all day long, following up one lead after another. Ten hours later, on their way home, they were tired but happy. They had seen car collections closed to all but a very few people.

18. HANGARS HOLD MORE THAN AIRPLANES.

My friend Peter Egan, long-time editor for *Road & Track*, wrote a column a number of years ago noting that private-plane pilots are often car enthusiasts as well. He noted a common mentality among pilots and car restorers—someone who enjoyed Piper Cubs might also enjoy Morgan sports cars and the like. At the time, Peter was a Piper Cub owner, so he spent time around small airports and noticed interesting cars stored under the wings of parked airplanes in the small hangers used by hobbyists. I decided to check out this aviation angle for myself; so while in Northern California's Napa Valley one weekend, I drove through a small airport. It was perfect weather for flying, so the hanger doors were wide open.

During that experiment, I saw an Austin-Healey Bugeye Sprite under the wings of one plane, a Mustang convertible under the wings of another, and an old Karman Ghia and a VW Beetle under another. Even though the planes looked to be well-maintained and regularly used, the cars often looked ignored and unused, leading me to believe they might be available for purchase.

19. TALK THE TALK; WALK THE WALK.

Shame on you if you are a car guy (or car girl) and don't let everyone you come in contact with know about your passion! Talk about your old car hobby with everyone you meet. If I am at a party, a wedding, even a funeral, people will learn that I'm a car person within minutes of meeting me. I have no desire to talk about "last week's NFL game" or some other time-wasting topic.

Depending on the party I'm attending, I'm either the most interesting or the most boring guy in the room.

It is my contention that EVERYBODY knows somebody with an old car. It might be their son's car he drove to college, the wretched wreck in their neighbor's backyard, or maybe their father-in-law's Model T that hasn't been driven in decades. Most people are not programmed to appreciate old cars and see them only as clutter taking up space in a garage. I find that the average non-car enthusiast is often curious as to why anyone would be interested in searching for cars that haven't run in years. Remember, to most people, cars are simply appliances. But if you explain your passion and give them a phone number or email address, you just might be surprised with a call a few days later.

I have two friends in my little town of Davidson, North Carolina, Hugh and Bruce. They are both car guys, who had known one another other for at least twenty-five years. But Hugh didn't know that Bruce still owned the Jaguar XK120 Roadster he had bought in 1955, and Bruce didn't know that Hugh owned the AC Greyhound coupe he had bought in the mid-1960s! I was the one who "introduced" them to each other as a fellow car guy. And both of them were shocked.

Don't let this happen to you! Make sure everyone in your family, neighborhood, town, clubs, and place of employment know that you pay homage to the car Gods.

20. TOWING AND STORAGE YARDS.

Where does a car enthusiast keep his or her cars when there is no more room at home? These days, the answer is easy: at one of the thousands of storage facilities that seem to blanket the countryside. Some storage businesses allow for outdoor storage, making it easy to spot cars, usually sitting along the back fence. The better cars are those sitting "inside" an actual storage unit, sometimes in a climate-controlled environment. The larger units are usually ten-feet wide and twenty-feet long, allowing for full-size American cars . . . or several classic Mini Coopers.

In an early *Barn Find Hunter* episode we filmed in Michigan, I followed up a lead about a rare 1967 Ford Country Squire station wagon that was resting in a storage facility. Fortunately, I was able to contact the owner (who had relocated to New York City) and receive permission to enter the unit. There sat the wagon, a huge land-yacht of a car, neatly stuffed into the metal storage building.

Again, here's where X-ray glasses would come in handy. Who knows how many cars are hibernating behind those darned metal doors. I suppose asking the facility manager if there were any unusual cars stored on the premises might work—or not.

Towing yards are also ripe with available cars. Towing companies are regularly called to clean out a garage or backyard, clean up property in order to put it for sale, or perhaps to settle an estate after the death of the owner.

Many times, those cars are brought directly to a crusher, but owners of towing companies are not stupid; if a car is interesting and has sale potential, they might just bring it back to their yard and sit on it for a while.

Recently, I visited a Pull-A-Part facility near my home. It's a salvage yard where a home mechanic can purchase and remove parts from soon-to-be-crushed cars. Before cars are picked apart, they are usually parked near the front office in the hopes that someone will buy the complete car as-is. During that recent visit, I saw an Alfa Romeo Spider and a Porsche 914, both of which were one hundred percent complete, but because they had probably been parked for a couple of decades in somebody's backyard, pretty rusty. Nonetheless, either car would have made an excellent parts car.

21. LAWYERS CAN BE YOUR FRIEND (REALLY!).

If you have a lawyer or a friend who is a lawyer, tell them to keep in mind that you are an old car enthusiast. Lawyers regularly settle the estates of the recently deceased. If there are assets cluttering up a piece of real estate—old cars in the garage or in the backyard, for example—they must be disposed of before the property can be sold. If your lawyer friend knows you are a collector, it might allow you to submit a bid for the car(s).

22. ESTATE SALES/AUCTIONS.

Check the local papers for estate sales or auctions in your area. Often necessitated upon the death or relocation of the home's occupant, a person's entire life is gathered on folding tables and offered to the public. You may have to spend the morning sifting through a porcelain doll collection and piles of antiquated hand tools, but sometimes "Uncle Fester" had a small collection of old Chevy trucks that must also be liquidated. Plus, it's a way to meet neighbors and spread the word that you are on the lookout for old cars.

23. BUSINESS CARDS.

Print business cards that state you are an old car enthusiast interested in old car projects. You can place these cards on old cars you see in parking lots and car shows. You can also leave these cards inside the screen doors of homes where an old car is visible and the homeowners are not home.

I still own the 1953 Ford Ranch Wagon I bought in 1972. I bought it for eighty-five dollars when I was a senior in high school. I spotted the two-door wagon while walking through the parking lot at a local department store where it was parked and fell in love. I left a note under the windshield, never expecting to hear back from the owner. But a few hours later, I received a call and the car was mine in no time. This method works, but no guarantee on finding an eighty-five dollar car these days.

24. GO POSTAL!

Mail carriers know every crack in the pavement, especially those walking from house-to-house with a mailbag hanging from their shoulder. They know who receives *Hemmings Motor News* and who potentially has old cars in their driveway or backyard. It can't hurt to talk to a couple of postal carriers and ask who on their route might be an old car enthusiast. Paying a "finder's fee" could certainly get their attention.

25. MECHANIC LIENS.

My friend Keith Irwin owns an old car shop that does maintenance, upgrades, and complete restorations. Keith does all the work on my old cars, especially my 1939 Ford Woody and my 1952 Cunningham C-3 coupe. I'll walk through the lot behind his shop, leading me to ask why the 1940 Ford coupe or 1953 Chevy sedan or whatever he had been working on in his shop is suddenly sitting outdoors.

The answer is never the same but the circumstances are always similar: the customer lost his job, he's financially over his head, he's ill, getting a divorce, decided to concentrate on another project, and so on. Whatever the reason, these once prized projects are suddenly put out to pasture and often available for purchase. So, check out restoration shops for someone else's project that may have gone belly-up.

A Mechanic's Lien is an official document of ownership that entitles the shop to recover delinquent repair costs on a car when the car's owner is no longer around or alive or has simply lost interest. Going through the proper channels, a car can be purchased with a clear title this way.

26. CELEBRITY TIP! GET YOUR OWN SHOW!

Jay Leno, America's most famous old car guy, had the best barn find gig going: when he hosted *The Tonight Show* for almost twenty years, all he'd have to do is mention an old car and the next day the phone in his Burbank business office was ringing off the hook! It was a platform like no other in the world; his millions of viewers, many of whom were elderly and had enjoyed his show for years, offered Jay cars that had inhabited their garages for years. Often, these cars were "rusty four-door Chevy Novas," as he is fond of saying. But sometimes, there were gems.

"If I'm interested, I always pay market value for these cars," he told me, "because I don't want to be seen as the rich guy who takes advantage of the poor widow." That's a good policy.

Wayne Carini, host of *Chasing Classic Cars*, also has a terrific platform with a show that directly targets old car enthusiasts.

As host of Hagerty's *Barn Find Hunter*, I regularly receive leads about old cars. Our program regularly attracts more than one million enthusiasts, most of whom are "tuned-in" to the barn find phenomenon. Most of the time I don't pursue these leads, instead preferring to hunt old cars the old-fashioned way. Since I was a kid, I've enjoyed cruising up and down streets and asking for suggestions at repair shops and auto parts stores. I know it's a harder way to find cars in today's digital world, but I think it's more authentic and honest. Anyone can answer the phone, get an address, and "discover" an old car, but I enjoy the "hunt" as much as the "discovery."

But for you, maybe it's not too late to go to acting school or become a comedian. If you get your own gig, maybe you, too, can talk about old cars the rest of us only dream about! It worked for Jay!

27. BONUS TIP! DON'T BE AN OLD FART!

For several years, I was an adjunct professor at a local Catholic college in North Carolina, Belmont Abbey College, where I taught motorsport public relations, marketing, and news writing. I gained experience in these subjects based on twenty-five years in the racing industry. But I was the dinosaur in the room when I brought in newspapers and realized that most of the students had never seen one. I was past my prime.

It's the same thing with hunting for old cars. Sure, I enjoy riding up and down country roads and knocking on doors when I see an old car in the driveway because it's an opportunity to travel, see pleasant sights, and meet neat people. But it's easier to use the keyboard that is likely sitting right in front of you, especially if you are looking for an old race car or show car that might have been featured in a magazine. There is no better way to track down old owners or trace a car's path than on the Internet. There are folks right now who are scouring the Web searching for old cars that have been out of the public eye for generations. There are lots of dead ends, for sure, but all you need is one hit and your time was well spent.

5

THE BARN FIND

AUTHOR

efore I wrote *The Cobra in the Barn*, I had no idea there would be an audience for such an obscure subject. But twenty years before I wrote that book, I had read with great fascination a story in an issue of the late *Automobile Quarterly* (Second Quarter 1984), called "Sleeping Beauties." It was heavy on photographs and light on copy and even lighter on facts. But still, I was captivated.

The automotive subjects were rare and beautiful art deco–styled cars that were being held prisoner on an estate somewhere in France: Bugatti, Tatra, Lancia, Panhard, Alfa Romeo, Lotus, Bentley, Jaguar, even an American Cord L29 and a supercharged Graham Paige. The cars, probably two dozen, had been left for nature to reclaim in an ashes-to-ashes scenario.

When this issue of *Automobile Quarterly* arrived in my mailbox in 1984, it rocked my world! I had long been a fan of the "Vintage Tin" column in *Rod & Custom*, but that column had long been discontinued. This gave me my first idea that perhaps I was not the only enthusiast interested in hidden cars. *Tom Cotter Collection*

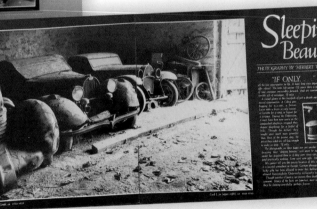

The story, "Sleeping Beauties," showed a secret stash of amazing and rare automobiles hidden on a farm somewhere in France. It was the owner's desire to leave the cars to deteriorate undisturbed back into the ground. Some thought it was an amazing art project. Others were furious. I was somewhere in the middle. *Tom Cotter Collection*

German photographer, Herbert Hasselman, did an amazing job of bringing beauty and intrigue to this polarizing scene. The opening paragraphs were obviously written without the benefit of many facts, so the editor was forced to write from an "Imagination" standpoint. The amazing photos told the story, however, with captions only identifying each car and little more.

Rust, spiderwebs, filth, broken glass—I believe many collectors protested that these valuable cars had been left to rot and were not being restored. But in an almost perverse way, I loved what I saw—the ultimate automotive sculpture, albeit one evolving very slowly, "Never to be awakened by the restorer's kiss," as the text said.

The story told of an owner, then an old man, who had acquired many of the cars for free, or very little money, decades earlier. It was during a time when people only viewed them as old cars and not automotive works of art. So the owner, who appreciated what they once had been, acquired them fearing that otherwise they would be brought to a junkyard and scrapped or dismantled.

Eventually, a book was written by three European enthusiasts—the Dutch father and son team of Ard op de Weegh and Arnoud op de Weegh and German Kay Hottendorff—who collectively unearthed much of the backstory. These three had been granted access to the collection where many others failed. They interviewed the collection's aging owner, who explained how and why he had obtained the cars.

Rather than recount the entire story here, I encourage you to purchase the book, *The Fate of the Sleeping Beauties*, published by Veloce in 2010. It's an interesting read and contains many intriguing photographs.

Before the article "Sleeping Beauties," I hadn't seen anything written about forgotten and neglected cars (the term *barn find* had not yet entered our vocabulary) since those old issues of *Rod & Custom* magazine's "Vintage Tin" feature. But, here was something new that told me I might not be the only one interested in rusty old cars.

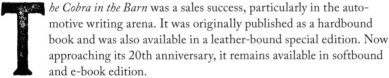

The Cobra in the Barn was a sales success, particularly in the automotive writing arena. It was originally published as a hardbound book and was also available in a leather-bound special edition. Now approaching its 20th anniversary, it remains available in softbound and e-book edition.

The format was simple: I wrote several personal stories about my own car-hunting experiences and combined those with stories and photos I had solicited from other folks with interesting tales to share. I asked my friend Peter Egan to write the foreword for the book. He did an amazing job, bringing deep insight into a subject he knew was my passion. He concluded with a sentence that sums it all up: "For a car guy, finding an old car is like meeting God."

Amen.

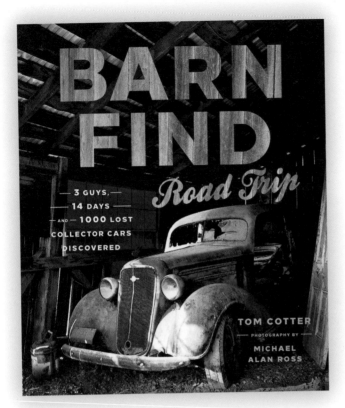

The success of *The Cobra in the Barn* led to of five similar books: *The Hemi in the Barn*, *The Corvette in the Barn*, and two motorcycle barn find books, *The Vincent in the Barn* and *The Harley in the Barn*. Collectively, these books have been well received by enthusiasts, many of whom have contacted me to tell me of their own finds. The format—my stories plus those of other collectors, all punctuated by "discovery day" photos—remained the same for all titles. It was a lot of fun, and sales were good across the series. Eventually, I tired of that format, however, and changed it to something that took me from behind my desk and put me behind the wheel.

Barn Find Road Trip was a new way to present the barn find experience to readers, and it put me on the spot to discover all of the featured old cars myself. The plan was this:

Eventually changing the format of my barn finding books, I wrote *Barn Find Road Trip*, about hitting the road and actually finding cars in real time. It was two great weeks with my friends Michael Alan Ross and Brian Barr. We met some terrific people and found amazing cars. *Tom Cotter Collection*

my barn finding buddy, Brian Barr, my favorite automotive photographer, Michael Alan Ross, and myself would spend two weeks driving around four states looking for old cars. The states we chose were Virginia, West Virginia, Maryland, and Pennsylvania. I did not include my home state, North Carolina, because I didn't want to be criticized for "finding" cars that I already knew about.

To add an interesting twist, we decided to take my 1939 Ford Woody instead of a more modern car. And it was on that trip I discovered a key barn finding tip revealed in the previous chapter: driving an interesting old car makes it easier to find other interesting cars. The car was always a conversation piece that opened up many opportunities to inspect cars that we normally never would have found.

The sales success and enthusiasm that *Barn Find Road Trip* produced meant another book of a similar format soon followed. *Route 66 Barn Find Road Trip* had the same crew— Brian, Michael, and I—once again in my intrepid Woody. This time, we drove from the Eastern Terminus of Route 66 in downtown Chicago all the way to the Santa Monica Pier in California, as the song goes: "More than 2,000 miles all the way."

The mission: we would search for old cars that: 1) sat along Route 66; 2) were visible from Route 66; or 3) were cars we had heard about while driving along Route 66. We found a bunch, hundreds, actually thousands if you include the amazing junkyard in Coffeeville, Kansas.

These books were so much fun to create, I felt like pinching myself.

We took one more road trip in the Woody, the last one to Detroit.

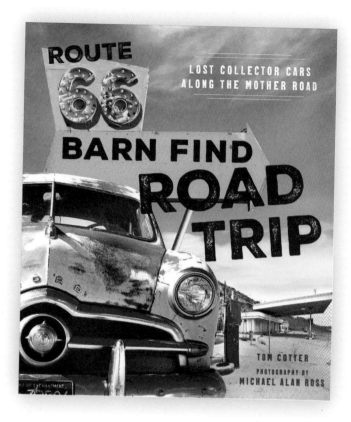

I figured nothing could be more American than to search for old cars in the birthplace of America's automobile industry. *Motor City Barn Find Road Trip* proved super interesting for an automotive history buff like me. In addition to finding amazing cars, many times owned by retired automotive executives, engineers, and factory workers, I also decided to make the book something of a travel guide for other enthusiasts who might want to follow in our tracks. We visited Ford's Rouge Assembly Plant, Henry and Clara Ford's gravesite, the original sites of specialty car builders Car Kraft and Dearborn Steel Tubing, Murray Body Corporation, the Ford Airport, and numerous other sites.

That Detroit trip also unearthed the one-of-one 1967 Ford Country Squire station wagon I mentioned earlier. I followed a lead to a storage facility near Ann Arbor, fell I love with the car, and bought it a few months later. If you've ever watched *Barn Find Hunter* on YouTube, you may remember that wonderful old Ford with just the right amount of patina. After enjoying the car for a number of years, I sold it on Bring a Trailer. The BaT post produced more than 700 comments!. A lot of people loved that car.

It's a big country, and I probably could have continued with the *In the Barn* and *Road Trip* series, but Hagerty came knocking with an interesting video series concept . . .

The next book in my road trip series was to find cars along Route 66. My traveling pals Michael Alan Ross and Brian Barr joined me in the Woody, and we drove from Chicago to Los Angeles on the old Mother Road. We made some great discoveries along the way. *Tom Cotter Collection*

MY BARN FINDS

LOTUS ELAN

I have been on the Advisory Board for McPherson College in Kansas for about ten years. If I were younger, I would enroll there. Why? Because they are the only college in the United States to offer a bachelor's degree in Automotive Restoration.

Students enroll in a four-year program where they split time between courses like history, science, and accounting, with shop courses such as engine rebuilding, sheet metal fabrication, and upholstery. Graduating students have the essentials to start their own restoration business. Others work for classic car auction houses, muse-ums, and private collections.

While on campus a few years ago, one of the automotive restoration professors, Brian Martin, asked me, "Hey, you're into small sports cars, right?" I told him yes though it is hard to believe that I prefer squeezing my almost six-foot, three-inch body into the cock-pit of small sports cars.

"I thought about you other day when a woman from town called asking if we knew of anyone who might be interested in her late father's Lotus Elan," Brian said. "If you'd like, I can show you the car during the lunch break today."

Sometimes, I find old cars, and sometimes, they find me! I quite unexpectedly stumbled across this Lotus Elan while attending a college board meeting at McPherson College in Kansas. Here it is being unloaded at my house during my annual car party. *Jordan Lewis*

Friends Keith Irwin (right) and Tom Farrell immediately jumped on the Lotus, which had been parked since the 1970s, and got the little twin-cam engine running within three hours. *Jordan Lewis*

As of this printing, the Lotus has been totally disassembled, the body has been soda blasted (photo), the chassis has been restored, and the engine is at the rebuilder. *Tom Cotter*

We drove to a warehouse on the industrial side of McPherson, an otherwise picturesque little berg in the Great Plains. We met with the woman, who guided us through an eclectic maze of stuff her dad had acquired over the course of his lifetime.

"My father died a year ago and I am trying to dispose of these items so I can sell the building," she explained. We passed a disorganized and cluttered mass of machinery, equipment, and electronics. We even passed a small Ford Ranger pickup truck that her father had attempted to convert to electric power. Interesting, but not my style.

When we arrived at the Lotus, it looked better than I thought it would. His daughter knew nothing about the car and could find no paperwork or ownership papers but believed it had been parked sometime in the 1970s. It looked complete, although dirty with the grime only a warehouse can produce.

I told her I was interested, and we discussed a price which I thought was fair but I told her she must apply for a lost title before I would buy it.

A couple of months later she sent a note that she had a title, and because the warehouse was about to be sold, she was ready to see it go to its new owner.

I convinced a couple of McPherson students to trailer the car to my house in North Carolina. That Fall, during my annual car party, I challenged a few of my car buddies to attempt to get the car running in two hours. It actually took three, but video exists of me driving the car around my driveway with a friend sitting on the floor next to me with an outboard-motor gas tank as he pumped fuel into the carburetors. A third friend sat on the front fender and manned the throttle while one more friend sat on the rear deck operating a video camera. Four people in an Elan! Colin Chapman was likely rolling over in his grave.

As of this writing, the car is disassembled in my garage, the engine is at the rebuilders, the chassis is waiting for some minor welding, and all the other parts have been restored and sit waiting on the shelf. I am having so much fun working on this car: it is small and simple. I hope to have it completed in the next twelve to eighteen months or about the time you are reading this book.

6

BARN FIND HUNTER

VIDEO
SERIES

Little did I know when I begged and borrowed the $300 to buy my 1939 Woody that it would still be part of my life a half-century later and a "Character" on my *Barn Find Hunter* series.

It pleases me no end that I am able to share that authentic barn find with the more than 1 million subscribers enjoying the *Barn Find Hunter* video series.

As I mentioned earlier, I received a call from Clair Walters of Hagerty in the fall of 2015 asking if they could follow along for a few days as my friends Brian Barr and Michael Alan Ross and I drove the Woody on the famous Route 66.

Neither the Hagerty video team, nor my car geek friends, knew what would happen. We stumbled with cameras, narration, and microphones—mostly me—but ultimately got the green light to produce a year's worth of videos to see if there was an appetite among the general public. The rest, as they say, is history.

Since its inception, the *Barn Find Hunter* series has covered at least half the United States, including Alaska (where there is surprisingly little rust!). And just before the world was shut down for the COVID-19 pandemic, we spent ten days searching for old cars in England (though the Woody stayed home for those episodes).

We all stumbled through the first pilot episode of *Barn Find Hunter*, as my soon-to-be Hagerty colleagues Clair Walters, Jordan Lewis, and Ben Woodworth trailed me for a couple of days as I was driving on Route 66 for another book. Obviously, it worked out, and now the program has more than one million subscribers!
Michael Alan Ross

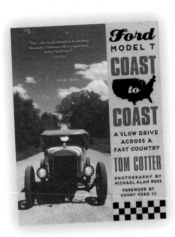

While driving a Model T across the United States for the book *Ford Model T Coast to Coast*, we stopped in Le Claire, Iowa, home of American Pickers. I was sad that it was little more than a souvenir store, with few collectible items available, and those that were, horribly overpriced. *Michael Alan Ross*

Many followers assume that I identify leads before arriving in an area to search for cars, but the reality is that I seldom enlist help for *Barn Find Hunter* episodes. I think mining for leads in context to the show is disingenuous, not authentic. It's certainly more clinical and less fun than the old fashion way of finding old cars. Plus, the name of the program is *Barn Find Hunter*, not *Barn Find Digital Database*.

Recently, there was a story in *The Charlotte Observer*, my hometown newspaper where I live in North Carolina. The headline stated that the *American Pickers* were coming to the Charlotte area in the near future, and that they were asking readers to "show us what you have." In other words, "before we travel to your city, send us photos of what you have so our advance team can survey your items, and we can negotiate the values and purchase arrangements before Frank and Mike arrive."

To me, this seemed so phony. The two guys driving around in the Antique Archeology Mercedes van weren't actually searching for anything, but simply following directions to a location with scripts in hand. *American Pickers* has an amazing national and international following, so their formula obviously works for them. But it's not the way I operate.

While driving a Model T across the United States for my book *Ford Model T Coast to Coast*, we stayed at a hotel located just a few miles north of *American Pickers'* headquarters in Le Claire, Iowa. Of course, we had to visit. Enroute to Le Claire, I imagined huge warehouses full of cool old stuff: cars, motorcycles, barber shop chairs, guitars—everything Mike and Frank searched out, negotiated, and purchased during their program. Boy, was I disappointed.

The Antique Archeology store and home base of the *American Pickers* TV show consisted of two small buildings that are now little more than souvenir shops. Collectible items were few and far between and were either NFS (Not For Sale) or overpriced junk. The buildings were mostly filled with new t-shirts, hats, and Mike Wolfe's line of leather jackets and belts. I was bummed. Here are two guys who have become famous for driving around the country buying cool old stuff, but their shop sells mostly new imported merchandise. I realize the show is entertainment, but my heart was broken.

All this led me to determine that *Barn Find Hunter* would be authentic. Therefore, I seldom use leads, but instead prefer to drive up and down streets, looking left and right. I stop at auto parts stores, body shops, and repair shops and ask the owners if they know of any old car guys in town. Then, I visit those folks and ask them if they know of other old car guys in the area and so forth. I've never failed in uncovering legitimate leads that will keep our film crew busy until it's time to fly home.

VIEW FROM THE
PASSENGER'S SEAT

by Jordan Lewis, Hagerty Videographer

Tom and I have driven over 35,000 miles, been to twenty-eight States, produced over one hundred episodes in five years, and never once have we come home empty handed. In this day and age, technology can make a lot of things easier, but just because it's easy doesn't mean you get the best results. When hunting for cars, Tom chooses to avoid technology and to pursue a more traditional route by driving down dead-end roads, dirt roads, and through industrial parks because this is how you find the gems never posted on the Internet. Tom's driving around approach is only half the battle, though. Starting a conversation and convincing an owner to let him see their most prized possessions is the most critical part of car hunting. Tom's success is all down to his uncanny ability to strike up a conversation with *any* car enthusiast, find common ground, and make that person realize their story matters.

I think it's only fitting to start off with a crazy story because this is how I was indoctrinated into the way of the *Barn Find Hunter*. It was just three days after meeting Tom on a cool fifty-degree November evening in a location just outside Gallup, New Mexico. We had had a prosperous day hunting cars in Gallup and figured we needed one more location to complete another episode, so we split town in hopes of finding one last location before calling it a day.

Jordan Lewis has been the codriver on nearly every episode of *Barn Find Hunter* since the series began in 2016. He has the rare dual talents of being a car guy, but more importantly, being a talented videographer and producer. *Ben Woodworth*

Our sunlight was limited, and we began to worry that we wouldn't find any cars. Suddenly, we rounded a bend and what do you know, there sat a yard with several muscle cars—Pontiac's to be specific. Now, this is where it gets sketchy. The property was a double wide trailer in the middle of the desert with a single mercury light overhanging the front gate that, of course, was attached to a fence surrounding the entire property.

During our first days filming *Barn Find Hunter*, we met with an anti-government hoarder. It was touch-and-go for a little while because he thought we were perhaps there to spy on him. At times like this, barn finding becomes dangerous. *Jordan Lewis*

Tom being the hound dog that he is, ignores these warning signs and is determined to get in. He finds there's no lock on the gate and nonchalantly opens it and begins to approach the trailer.

Let's pause for a second to let me paint a picture for you. This is my fourth week working for Hagerty on what was going to be the company's biggest production to date and here I am watching the star of our show approach a house that looks like it's straight out of *Breaking Bad*. Notice how I said the star—when Tom agreed to do the show with us, it was going to be done his way, with his rules, and his tactics, which meant he would always be the one to approach a house. On any other production, a producer would approach the property owner to explain their reason for stopping. He enthusiastically walks up and knocks on the door while I listen in on the microphone attached to Tom and the rest of the crew watches. From a distance, the

door cracks open and we are all watching intently, hoping that we aren't run off with a gun or a pack of dogs. The owner asks, "can I help you?" Tom lays down his classic line: "Hi, my name is Tom Cotter, and I drive around the country writing books and filming a series about finding old cars. I'm interested in any stories you have about that Pontiac LeMans." The gentleman looked down his driveway and saw two black SUVs, which would concern just about anybody, but then in front of the SUVs, was Tom's 1939 Ford Woody wagon. The Woody often serves as an icebreaker into a more friendly conversation, but this time it wasn't enough.

"Are you with the Government?" the property owner asked. Tom reassured him that we weren't. After a question like that, what does one say? Without skipping a beat Tom asks, "Does that Pontiac LeMans have a 215 or is it a 326? I saw it had wide tires in the rear and that you had cut a hole in the floor for a manual transmission." Immediately, Tom becomes more credible and the guy lets his guard down enough to step out and walk down to the cars with Tom. As Tom and the owner head toward the cars, he made it clear how private he was, "Just so you know, I don't carry a cell phone or a credit card . . . I'm a very private guy."

We were working our way through his collection one by one, and Tom was being patient and letting the guy tell him about the cars, which is another tactic Tom uses because letting a person talk about their cars can go a long way to gaining their trust. He reassured him, "I'm not here to buy anything, I just want to hear any stories you have about these cars or how you got into cars. I care about the stories more than the cars because these cars will be here long after we are all gone, but the stories won't."

Several years later, and not far from Gallup, New Mexico, we took a hop to St. George, Utah. We had been in town for three days and had had good success finding cars by driving around and attending a local Cars & Coffee. Every person that we had met over the past three days all spoke of one-man: Red Blake. Between all the stories we had heard about Red, the one thing that was consistent was that he was very grumpy and he didn't want to be bothered about his cars. If you did get in, you were walking on eggshells because one wrong word or one wrong look and you were kicked out. Every person told us something mysterious or crazy about Red, and as Tom heard each story, I could see him become more and more driven to find this man and hear his story.

Red owned a large salvage yard that through all his years of running a towing business had become jam-packed with rare, optioned vehicles

of all shapes and sizes. We were able to determine the location of Red's salvage yard, and we headed straight there in hopes of finding him before the business day was over. Arriving at the location, we found all the gates closed and a ten-foot tall, twelve-inch-thick concrete wall with barbed wire fence surrounding all forty-four acres of cars. In typical fashion, Tom begins some reconnaissance to try to find a back way in or find any way to see inside. With a little more searching, he was able to find a high spot about one hundred yards outside the wall that would allow him to see down into St. George's most mysterious car collection. While observing the wonderful treasure inside the yard, he spotted a crane dumping scrap into a crusher. In a last-ditch effort to draw someone's attention, Tom tried driving his Ford Woody over to the high ground hoping to catch Red's eye. Unfortunately, Red was a Chevy guy.

Now, there was only one thing left to do: leave the Mother of all voicemails. Tom pulled out all the stops and did everything he could to appeal to Red's better self by letting him know we were there to hear his story and not obsess over his cars. Nine times out of ten this is the line that gets our foot in the door, and it worked again. To shorten a long story, Tom did hear back from Red, and we were able to film and see Red's amazing collection.

There are many approaches to barn find hunting, and you can see how it might be easy to lean on technology from the comfort of your couch. But that takes away the fun of the pursuit and the dying art of carrying on a conversation.

Next time you are on the road and spot a diamond in the rough, don't be afraid to pull over, knock on the door, and have a good chat about old cars. Because at the end of the day, that's all any car person wants to do.

We were able to gain access into Red's, a salvage yard in St. George, Utah, after locals told us we'd never get inside the long-closed business. Red was a great guy and gave us complete run of his amazing yard, which included this AMC Pacer sculpture. *Jordan Lewis*

What kind of cars don't get my attention for our episodes? When we are searching for old cars, there are many I simply ignore. They fall into two categories: 1) extremely rusty cars that are literally returning to the earth or 2) cars that were manufactured half-heartedly by U.S. manufacturers during an era when they weren't really interested in manufacturing cars anyway.

To clarify the rusty car comment: If I pass a car "outstanding in its field" with no other cars or garages around it, I'll give it a little nod, but not stop. Now, if there is a barn or garage nearby, that rusty hulk might be a red herring and something more interesting exists inside. If that is my hunch, I'll be knocking on the door in a moment.

Now, about the half-hearted cars: There are cars that were produced by American car companies that were just crappy cars, specifically late 1970s and 1980s GM front-wheel-drive cars and Chrysler K-cars, both built during a period where car manufacturers took their eyes off the road. In that era, car companies were hiring brand managers from consumer product companies like Proctor & Gamble and General Foods who were more familiar with marketing toothpaste and laundry detergent. That's how disenfranchised Detroit was. Here's my beef: when GM decided to follow the VW Rabbit with front-wheel-drive platforms, its cars were an afterthought and not designed to provide a long-term, quality driving experience. The Oldsmobiles, Pontiacs, Buicks, and Chevrolets of that era were shoddily designed and built. What turned me off about the cars, and specifically GM as a leading manufacturer, was that when the U.S. Government issued a maximum 55 mph national speed limit, GM responded by "down-sizing" the brakes on new Chevy Citations to haul a car down from 55 mph max! To save a few pennies per car, the largest corporation in the world cheapened the brakes, of all things. This told me GM valued corporate profit way more than customer safety.

Don't write to tell me that the "high-performance" X11 version of the Citation had better brakes; I know that. I stand by my opinion regardless of the Hi-Po version.

Another instance of GM putting customers second was the redesign of the V-8 engine in the front-wheel-drive Oldsmobiles of the 1980s. In this case, they buried the starter motor in the valley beneath the intake manifold! It was actually ridiculous! A part as commonly changed as a starter motor suddenly became a job too complicated for a home mechanic to attempt and too expensive to bring to a dealer to repair. I think that's the reason so many of these cars had a short lifespan or are resting in fields where they remain ignored by all, including me.

Regarding the Chrysler K-car, what a ridiculous little car. Whether the two-door, four-door, or wagon, these cars were the cheapest of the cheap.

Anyway, if we're driving around in the Woody and see a field or driveway filled with American cars of that era, we just keep on driving.

My *Barn Find Hunter* cohost is my yellow 1939 Ford Woody. It takes the two of us to approach a possibly reluctant old car owner and get to first base. The Woody is my "icebreaker," a literal welcome wagon to discovering neglected and ignored collector cars.

If we're filming a *Barn Find Hunter* episode in the Southeast or Mid-Atlantic states, I'll just drive the Woody from my home in North Carolina to those areas. The car has been updated and easily cruises at highway speeds and offers modern creature comforts. But when filming is scheduled for the Northeast, Midwest, or West Coast, Hagerty pays to have the Woody shipped in an enclosed carrier to that location and I fly in to meet it.

I'm not afraid to drive the car over long distances—it's been driven cross-country several times—but the time required would be prohibitive. Plus, even though the drivetrain has been upgraded to an LS1 aluminum block Corvette engine with modern accessories, it's still an old car. It would prematurely wear out many of its original components. Even so, I bet the Woody is one of the most driven hot rods in the United States.

Selecting filming locations is a key part of our planning, though it's not complex. I sit down with my Hagerty colleagues and they ask, "Where do you want to go next?" In one instance, I answered, "Midland, Texas."

After referring to their iPhones to see where Midland is located, one of them wondered, "Why would you want to go to some town in rural west Texas?"

"Well, I've always wanted to see where Jim Hall built the Chaparral Can-Am race cars."

And that was it! Little did any of us know that our Midland, Texas, shoot would lead to one of the most popular and memorable episodes in our six years of filming!

In keeping with my precision planning, I would like for a future episode to be blindfolded and to then throw a dart toward a large wall map of the United States. No matter where the dart lands on the map, that's where we'll travel to see what cars might be hiding there.

We've also considered having our viewers enter a drawing with the prize being a visit to the winner's hometown to search for old cars. As a bonus, the winning viewer would be invited to join us during our hunt.

Or, maybe while flying to the West Coast, I'll look out the airplane's window, choose a random town below, and ask the flight attendant if they or the pilot could identify that town. Then, I'll travel back to that town and search for barn finds.

Lost cars are always on my mind. I often think about how many hundreds, or thousands, of hidden cars I must be flying over when commuting across our great country. There are undoubtedly cars that have been hidden in barns and garages, hidden from view for half a century or more. I'd like to find them all, of course, and the *Barn Find Hunter* is an excellent outlet for my obsession.

(OVERLEAF) How do we pick locations to film episodes? There's nothing scientific about it. We pretty much throw a dart on a map. The crew asks where I'd like to go next, and we go. We saw this scene in Midland, Texas, because I wanted to visit the town where Jim Hall built the fabulous Chaparral Can-Am race cars in the 1960s. *Jordan Lewis*

1962 FORD COUNTRY SEDAN WAGON

My *Barn Find Hunter* camera crew and I had just landed in Midland, Texas, a very blue-collar town loaded with oil-rich millionaires all driving jacked-up four-wheel-drive pickup trucks. I have been intrigued with the town for years because Chaparrals—some of the most innovative and exotic race cars ever constructed—were built there by driver and team owner Jim Hall.

As we would soon learn, the town was also loaded with barn find cars. A couple of hours after arriving there, I was driving around in the Woody when I passed a fenced in yard on the industrial side of town that was loaded with old cars, mostly Fords. I entered the shop adjacent to the yard and met the owner, Tom Cross, whose main business was installing in-ground swimming pools for those blue-collar, pickup-driving millionaires. But Tom's real passion is Fords of the 1960s.

"Sure, go back there with your cameras and spend all the time you need," said Tom, who has since become a good friend. "Those cars are the remainder of all the cars I dragged in from surrounding states years ago. I'm beginning to think about crushing them and selling the property."

I gravitated toward this 1962 Ford Country Sedan Wagon in Tom Cross' Midland, Texas, yard of project cars. It had lasted in the desert for decades, but I could tell the car didn't want to die. *Jordan Lewis*

I walked around, camera crew in tow, looking at the cars: a 1964 Ford Galaxie with a 390 cubic inch engine, some Falcons, a red 1962 Ford Country Sedan Wagon, a 1960 Ford two-door station wagon, along with literally dozens of other cars.

I kept going back to that 1962 Ford wagon. It seemed pretty solid, all the glass was in good shape, but it had no drivetrain and the interior was blown out. Still, it seemed to have good bones.

We walked around filming for another hour or so as I described what I saw. But I kept circling back to that wagon. The original paint, once a brilliant red, had faded to a dusty pink after decades in the desert sun. I remember a TV commercial from when I was a kid—maybe it was for Simoniz or J-Wax—where a man walked up to a dingy car with faded paint in a junkyard and polished it to like-new condition. I have always wanted to do the same thing. Maybe this was my shot.

"Hey, Tom," I called to Cross, "might you have some compound and an old rag?" Within a couple of minutes, Tom was back with the supplies. For the next fifteen minutes, I rubbed and rubbed and rubbed that paint. The small ten-inch by ten-inch piece of metal shined like new paint— amazing for a car over fifty-years-old.

"I wish I had a buffer," I said to Tom, never thinking he might actually had one in his shop.

"I have one, but not enough extension cord to reach out here. But I have an idea," he said as he ran off toward the shop. A minute later, I heard a diesel engine rumbling to life across the yard. Then, I saw a tractor with a forklift coming our way. Tom moved a Rambler and another Ford that were in the way; then, he picked up the red station wagon and carried it back to his building. Within five minutes I had a buffing wheel, extension cord, liquid compound, and rags. I started buffing away with the cameras rolling. An hour later, the car's right front fender was "shining like a million bucks," as my Uncle Bob used to tell me when I polished his red Mustang.

I borrowed a bottle of paint compound and a rag and got an amazing shine out of the previously dull paint. That led to buying the car and Tom Cross, his friends, and family rebuilding the car from bumper-to-bumper. *Jordan Lewis*

"This car doesn't want to die," I declared, now hot, tired, and dirty with compound dust, yet satisfied with the amazing result.

One thing led to another, and Hagerty wound up buying the car. Cross said it could stay at his shop and he and his friends would continue to work on it. My original plan was to auction off the car, maybe on Bring a Trailer, with proceeds going to a charity. Then, an idea . . .

As noted earlier, I'm on the Advisory Board for McPherson College, a Kansas school that offers a bachelor's degree in Automotive Restoration. I knew their shop truck, a Chevy LUV, was on its last legs. Perhaps they could use this wagon. I called Amanda Gutierrez, the Vice President of the program, and she loved the idea. She even offered to have a couple of students come down to Texas and help work on the car over winter break.

One year later, we drove the rebuilt wagon 1,000 miles, from Midland, Texas, to McPherson, Kansas, and donated it to McPherson College's Automotive Restoration Technology Program. It was an amazing journey from beginning to end. You should catch it on YouTube. *Jordan Lewis*

Thank goodness Cross and his friends did more than their share of work because there was a lot to do, and I lived 1,200 miles away. I made a couple of trips to Midland over the course of the next year, working with the McPherson students and also Hagerty dynamo Brad Phillips, who is a hands-on executive. Over the course of twelve months, that junkyard dog was transformed into a really sweet driver. Cross and his local team rebuilt and installed a sweet 390 with a four-barrel carburetor, rebuilt Ford-O-Matic transmission, Mexican blanket interior, new suspension, disc brakes, dual exhaust, and scores of other improvements.

The following May, about fourteen months after first stumbling across this wagon, we drove it for a couple of *Barn Find Hunter* episodes enroute to delivering it to McPherson, about 1,000 miles away.

The restoration students welcomed us with a hot dog cookout, and all the restoration professors were eager to see what we had been working on for all those months. The school's President, Michael Schneider, gladly accepted the keys to his school's new/old wagon.

It was one of the best *Barn Find Hunter* shows we had ever filmed and all because we decided to get off the beaten path to Midland, Texas.

Good cars are hiding everywhere.

Viewers often assume that I buy all the cars I find. Invariably, the first question they'll ask is, "What do you do with all the cars you buy on the program?"

The answer is easy: I don't buy any. Or, not many, anyway.

I prefer a more "documentary" approach when searching for old cars: find the car, meet the owner, hear the story, and then move on.

I have bought hundreds of cars in my life, and I always have too many stuffed in my garage. I don't need more cars (well, except maybe sometimes . . .), and my wife would not be enthusiastic about any new acquisitions. Recently, I had twenty-one cars between my garage and a storage warehouse, but I've been selling cars and hope to get my car-count down to around ten in the near future.

But the *Barn Find Hunter* does offer temptations. A recent exception was the 1967 Ford Country Squire wagon whose story I recounted in the previous chapter.

After I found that car, I called Pat and told her I needed to own it. Three months later, after a bit of negotiating both with Adrian and Pat, it was mine. If you are a *Barn Find Hunter* regular, you will certainly recall that I used the Country Squire rather than the Woody on a number of episodes. It was such an interesting car to drive. People in other cars either thought I was homeless and urged their children not to stare or thought I was the

Okay, sometimes even the *Barn Find Hunter* falls in love . . . I had to own this V-8 powered Rambler Marlin with a factory four-speed gearbox. And it ran! Sadly, when I inspected it at home, it was rougher than I had hoped, so I traded it to friend Keith Irwin. *Jordan Lewis*

hippest dude on the planet. I certainly got odd looks when I drove the car to Kansas with a surfboard on the roof. Still, it was one of the cars I decided to sell during my recent garage sale, so it has gone off to a new, appreciative owner.

The only other *Barn Find Hunter* car I have bought followed an episode we had filmed in South Carolina and northern Georgia. The owner of a large stash of interesting cars—including a 1954 Corvette—had one car that got my attention: a Rambler Marlin. I've always liked Rambler Marlins, but this one was powered by a V-8 engine—287 cubic inches if I remember correctly—and was a factory four-speed car. And it ran! I asked him how much, the price was more than fair, so I bought it.

He delivered it a week later, and I gave the car a close inspection as it sat in my driveway. As I lay on the ground looking up through the left front fender, I could see the car's headliner. That was not a good sign. I called my friend Keith to look at it. The firewall had enough rust that it had partially separated from the cowl, which allowed me to see the headliner from the ground.

Clearly, I had made a mistake, so I asked Keith if he knew anyone who might be interested in the car for the same price I had paid.

"I like this car," he replied. "I'm interested."

We did a deal right there: I gave him the Marlin and he painted the Datsun 510 I was in the process of restoring. Keith owns Keith Irwin Restorations and has the ability and tools to repair the Marlin, which he hopes to restore.

No barn find error is beyond redemption.

L ike you, I have watched all the "junkyard" shows on TV. You know the setup: two guys walk through a junkyard pointing out certain cars and discussing how cool it would be to get them running again. Some shows even repair those cars and drive them out after a "couple of days" off thrashing. I'm glad the hosts of those shows enjoy themselves and that there is an audience for that content, but it's not for me.

After many years of writing about old cars, I realize that I am a storyteller. The car is only a catalyst in delivering a human-interest story, which is where the real interest lies. Cars in a commercial junkyard have little to tell. To the junkyard owner, those cars are simply inventory to be sold, parted out, or scrapped.

The *Barn Find Hunter* focuses on individual car owners as they can weave tales of how they acquired the car with their paper route money or were given the car upon graduation by their spinster aunt. Those are the stories I love to unearth and share with my viewers when I can draw them from an owner.

Let it be forever known that I would rather "discover" one old car with an interesting story than stumble across 1,500 cars in a field.

One of the highlights, just before the COVID-19 pandemic stopped the world as we know it, was filming episodes in England. Here is my friend Cliff Ryan (right) and his son Sam, showing off his beautifully restored Austin 35. *Jordan Lewis*

Believe it or not, rare cars like R-Code Galaxies still exist out there! Keep hunting. *Michael Alan Ross*

I regularly see comments posted on various *Barn Find Hunter* episodes where viewers say something like:

"Too many foreign cars. Why doesn't Tom concentrate on more Mopars?"

"Why do you always find Fords? Please find more GM muscle cars."

"Please try to find a 427 Yenko Chevelle. I've always wanted one."

Consider this, which may burst your bubble but should be obvious by now: I have no idea what awaits me behind any barn door. When I get a lead about an old car, I won't know what I'll find until I get there and see it with my own eyes. It is virtually impossible to hunt for a particular type of car, especially something as specific as a 427 or Hemi-powered rig.

Sometimes, I find alloy bodied Ferraris, and sometimes, I find rusty Corvairs. I have no power to change that unless I throw out the authenticity of the program. I could send out a social media bulletin announcing that I will be coming to a certain area and that I'll be looking for a certain brand or type of car, say an R-code (427CI) Ford Galaxie or an L88 Camaro. That's not gonna happen. The *Barn Find Hunter* will continue to ply his trade the old-fashioned way of seeking old cars, with my tried and true approach. I truly enjoy unearthing cars and presenting them to the viewers as I found them, not pretending to find cars that have been prearranged.

It's called "hunting," remember.

ever has the varied condition of old cars been so obvious than when we hit the road in 2015 for the book *Route 66 Barn Find Road Trip*. Departing from the Eastern Terminus of Route 66 in Chicago, near the western shore of Lake Michigan, we probably passed numerous old cars on that cold, windy Sunday morning. But we didn't look, and we didn't stumble across any. There were two reasons: 1) It was early on a Sunday morning, traditionally the worst time of the week to go knocking on doors; and 2) Chicago is a big city with lots of skyscrapers, which means it takes lots of time to discover cars there. And we just didn't have a lot of time.

California, here we come!

A couple of hours down the road, in the suburbs south of Chicago, old cars along the Mother Road were highly visible. That Sunday morning we found pickup trucks, 1957 Chevys, and VW buses sitting behind body shops and in people's backyards. Most were restorable, but at what cost?

If a restorer is a proficient welder and fabricator, anything can be brought back to life. But in my experience, it is very difficult, expensive, and time consuming to rebuild a car with bad bones.

As we continued south and west over the course of the next two weeks, the cars sitting outdoors began to look better and better. Relics in Missouri were in somewhat better condition than those in Illinois. The cars in Oklahoma were better than those one state north in Kansas. And when we found cars in Texas, New Mexico, Arizona, and Southern California, the cars were considerably better than in more easterly states.

Sure, old cars in the Southwest were usually covered in surface rust and their interiors were usually blown out because the threads and fabrics dry up and fall apart. But the "bones" of those cars—the chassis, floors, rockers, and body panels—were far superior to the cars we had seen just a few days earlier in Illinois.

Which leads me to this somewhat obvious advice: If you live in the northern regions of the United States, get in your car and drive to the Southwest. You will forever be thankful that you dragged home a car with good bones instead of paying someone one hundred dollars per hour to resurrect them.

(OPPOSITE)
This wonderful Art Deco Nash, discovered in the eastern California desert, was rock solid and had nothing but surface rust. I fell in love with this car and dreamed of an LS drivetrain, but alas, NOT FOR SALE. *Michael Alan Ross*

(OVERLEAF)
Cars in the northern United States, if kept outdoors, are rough. I know; I grew up in New York. My suggestion when car hunting in the north is to concentrate on cars stored indoors. Otherwise, go south! *Michael Alan Ross*

FARMERS NEVER SELL

One thing I have learned from talking to farmers while driving and searching for old cars in the Great Plains is that cars and trucks there live long and useful, practical lives. When those vehicles get old, they are seldom scrapped or sold. Instead, they are simply towed by tractor into the "back 40" and parked next to all the other cars where they serve a new and practical life: wind breaks.

Wind break? Yes. After the winds blew all the good soil eastward during the 1930s, turning the Midwest into the Dust Bowl, farmers had to get smarter about designing their fields to prevent their livelihoods from blowing away. So, they began planting trees perpendicular to the prevailing easterly winds in an effort to slow down the gusts. They told me that old vehicles are parked in rows not only to cut the winds, but also act as shelters allowing vegetation to take root and making it possible for trees to grow better.

This explains why you may notice old cars parked in neat rows, half buried in sand and soil, sitting among lines of trees; after decades of doing their jobs as wind breaks, the cars become a backstop for airborne dirt. Often, though, these cars are beyond redemption, having been exposed to constant sandblasting and the harshest weather for years or decades. Sometimes, though, hard parts and trim might be worthy of harvesting.

Farmers also hold onto old cars because they are homegrown engineers and mechanics, constantly in need of spare parts to quickly repair a truck or tractor. This is a priority when you live many miles from the nearest auto parts stores or junkyard. These cars are often as good as having an auto parts store on the property.

Another thing you may notice: more than a few farmers are also hot rodders and racers, so parts from these deceased vehicles may eventually find themselves in a sportier ride.

There was a time when I wanted to buy every old car I found, especially if it was a desirable Ford from the 1930s or 1940s. When I was younger, I usually had some money and storage space, and I was almost guaranteed I could turn it for a profit upon resale. Understand that I have never dealt in selling cars for a living, only as a hobby, so selling them was always Plan B. The problem has always been that I fall in love with my cars, and I want to keep them forever.

I have an ability to see "through" the rust, to imagine the beautiful car this barn find could become. It's called imagination, of which I seem to possess more than my share.

Over the past few years, especially since I began hosting *Barn Find Hunter*, I'm having more fun learning each car's story than considering ownership. I compare it to treasure hunting as a kid. I remember my friends and I digging a huge hole in the backyard of my boyhood home on Long Island, in an effort to make a tunnel to China. We figured that on the way to China, we were bound to find hidden pirates' treasure chests filled with gold and jewels.

See what I mean about imagination?

(Even as an adult, my mother told me I should go into the backyard and start digging, because she believed I lost many of my Dinky Toys in those dirt piles as a kid . . .)

Well, searching for old cars has, for me, become an adult version of childhood treasure hunting. But, the search has become the most satisfying aspect—following up leads, hitting the pavement, meeting people, and taking chances. That's the dramatic part. Acquisition becomes anticlimactic.

Consider it automotive foreplay.

In my case, the story becomes the treasure, and as you've already read here, I would rather sit and talk with the long-time owner of a car with an interesting story than stumble across a field of cars. Owners have stories; junkyards have inventory.

Sadly, cars can't talk, except in the rare instance when paperwork from a previous owner remains in the glovebox. Then, a piecing together of the car's life can become extremely rewarding—or imagined.

DATSUN 510 REDUX

By this point in the book, it's no secret that I'm a Datsun 510 freak. The cars, built between 1968 and 1973, were amazing deals, with BMW features like overhead cam engine, disc brakes, independent suspension, all wrapped up in an attractive package for $1,995 brand new! And 510s could easily be converted into road racers and rally cars capable of winning championships.

I once owned a repair shop that specialized in the brand, and I owned dozens of them when they were cheap and plentiful. But that's not the case anymore. Datsun 510 bodies were made of thin steel without any sort of rust proofing, so the cars basically deteriorated and were scrapped. This is why when I see one in someone's yard, I'm knocking on the door.

One 510, a rare 1968 four-door, was barely visible in a carport way off the road in a neighborhood near my house. I kept passing and noticed the car never moved. One day in, I think, 2005, I knocked on the door. The man who answered was slightly embarrassed because of the car's condition. He said it had been his daily driver, but then he got into Mopars and just parked it. His intention had been to modify it, but his tastes changed.

"Yeah, I'd sell it," he said.

We negotiated a price—eighty dollars—and I trailered it home the next day. The worst part about it was dealing with all the bee nests throughout the car. It sits in my warehouse today, bee free, awaiting restoration by someone else. I am concentrating on my 1972, and I don't need distraction.

Another 510 I stumbled across was a 1972 four-door that had been parked for decades in the yard of an uninhabited house. The car had sunk into the ground sitting just fifty feet from an empty garage. A shame, but, on the other hand, if it hadn't been parked outdoors, I never would have found it.

Anyway, I knocked on the next-door neighbor's door and learned that the house was owned by a woman who lived on the other side of town. Helpfully, the neighbor told me the woman's daughter was a schoolteacher at the local elementary school.

I drove immediately to the school and left a message for the woman with the school secretary. Eventually, she called me and gave me her Mom's phone number. That began a dialogue that lasted for several years.

I would call and leave a message, and she'd call me back six months later. When we did actually connect, she told me she had actually purchased the car brand new and had owned it since she graduated from high school in 1972!

She admired my sleuthing method of finding her through her daughter, but she was worried I wanted to scrap the car. I assured her that I was a collector and that would not be the case.

Eventually, several years after first discovering the car, we decided on a price of $500 and it was mine. When I picked up the car, the original owner stood in the yard and cried as she said goodbye to her baby. But she was pleased to see it go to someone who would not dismantle it.

She gave me a number of documents including the original bill of sale and the owner's manual.

The years of sitting outdoors sinking into the lawn had taken its toll on the already fragile car. But it has possibilities and should be restored to showroom condition by someone other than me.

As a long-time Datsun 510 enthusiast, I seldom see them "in the wild," mostly because they rusted so badly. When I found this one at a vacant house in North Carolina, though, I had to pursue it. After months, I finally found the owner, who grew up in the house. I was able to buy the car for $500 only after promising I would not strip it and sell it for parts. *Tom Cotter*

Here's the original owner, Carol Keeler, saying a tearful goodbye to the Datsun 510 she bought new after high school graduation in 1972 for $1,995. Sometimes, meeting the people and hearing their stories is more valuable than the car. *Tom Cotter*

8

HIDING
IN PLAIN SIGHT
(UNLESS YOU LOOK)

When Pat and I decided to buy a cottage in our favorite vacation spot, Boothbay Harbor, on the Maine seacoast, I realized I'd be leaving my passion for searching for old cars during the four months we planned to spend there each summer. Maine is largely rural, with many long-time seasonal residents, older houses, and quaint villages, so I'm sure there are lots of old cars to be found in that huge state. But Boothbay Harbor is more of a seaside vacation town, with a somewhat younger, more transient population. While I was in town during the summer months, I figured I'd enjoy the scenery, food, and history, with plenty of time to read and write. I could always search the rest of the state when I needed a barn find fix.

Boy, was I wrong.

Soon after we arrived for our first summer there, in 2015, Pat and I attended a First Friday art tour, an art crawl around some of the studios and galleries in town. We walked quietly, wine glasses in hand, through each gallery as we looked at the paintings and sculptures. Then, I overheard a conversation on the other side of the room at one gallery.

In a garage just a half-mile from my Maine cottage sits Bob McKay's amazing and rare Lotus 11. The aluminum-bodied car was first campaigned in the 1,000-mile Mille Miglia in 1957. *Tom Cotter*

"So, I downshifted into third and took Big Bend at about half-throttle," said one man to another.

"Excuse me, Babe, but there is a conversation over there I need to be part of," I told Pat.

I wandered over, listened to the two men for a moment, then asked, "Are you guys talking about racing at Lime Rock?"

Lime Rock in a 1.5-mile road circuit in the northwest corner of Connecticut and my favorite place to race my Corvette.

"Why, yes, do you race there too?" asked one of the men.

One thing led to another, and I was invited to visit one gentleman's garage, just a half-mile from my house. The next day, I walked over and he led me into the garage. There he showed me his daily driver, the Ferrari 308 he had purchased new. Next, he lifted a canvas cover off the car parked in front of a driver-quality MG TD, which he used regularly. In front of that, he uncovered the *creme d'la crème*, a 1955 Lotus XI, a voluptuous aluminum-bodied sports racer complete with its original Coventry Climax engine.

"Colin Chapman [Lotus founder] drove this one himself in the 1955 Mille Miglia," my new friend told me.

He showed me a photo of the car in that race. In that picture, the car was fitted with a full windshield and headlights, but the car in front of me had a small racing windscreen and no headlights, just aluminum covers. When I asked about those items, he pointed to the shelf behind the car, where a full windscreen and two headlight units sat.

Here's some of the famous folks who drove Mckay's Lotus in period. Even Lotus founder, Colin Chapman, entered the car in Sprint races in the United Kingdom. *Tom Cotter*

Gregor Grant 1957 Mille Miglia
Cliff Allison
Innes Ireland
Colin Chapman

"I took those off so they wouldn't get damaged when I vintage raced the car back in the 1980s," he explained. The last time he raced the car was in the 1989 Meadowlands Grand Prix.

"It's been sitting in this garage ever since."

Amazing. This was a substantial piece of racing history just a half-mile from my home in a town I thought would contain no barn finds. Six years later, the car still hasn't moved one inch.

Since then, I've discovered a 1970 MGB in a garage just two houses from mine; an MGA roadster—still with the same owner since 1970—in a garage at the next corner; and a 1972 Ford Bronco two streets away.

"My father bought that Bronco new in '72," the owner told me. "When he passed, he left it to me. It only has 27,000 miles on the odometer."

These finds and new friendships are great examples of my earlier point that one of the best ways to discover hidden cars is to always be listening in social situations and to be sure everyone knows you are a car guy. Old cars are all over, even in coastal vacation towns that "presumably" have no old cars.

VIEW FROM THE
PASSENGER'S SEAT

by Michael Alan Ross

Professional photographer Michael Alan Ross and I have collaborated on five books together, spending weeks on the road each time. He covers the visual side of my barn finding adventures with fantastic photos of the cars I find.

After thousands of miles, experiencing Tom Cotter's obsession for discovering barn finds firsthand, I've made a few observations.

Tom is nonstop, from sunup 'till sundown, in his quest to discover these hidden treasures. He has a built-in radar and a knack for being able to recognize them by simply seeing a shadow on the wall or a peeking tail lamp.

I often refer to him as "the truffle hunting dog of rust." His instincts are superhuman when it comes to finding rotting metal. His peripheral vision is so keen, he can almost see around corners. I'd swear his neck swivels 180 degrees like the seats in a '61 Buick Flamingo. How he can do that and drive straight, I will never know.

Tom tends to gravitate to that part of town where folks might get away with parking cars on their front lawn for, oh, a few decades. His favorite technique is to prominently park his Woody (typically in a no parking zone) outside the local watering hole and find a seat at the bar. Inevitably, by his second beer, he will have come up with three possible locations where "Jimmy's got a few old cars around back of his place." Now granted, Jimmy may be long gone, and those cars may have been scrapped years ago, but it's that tip that will put him smack dab in the middle of where he needs to be.

When Tom arrives at a "find," he has a few rules. He insists on approaching, alone, with his hands always at his side with open palms. It's a sign he's hiding nothing. Once someone opens the door to their home, it's usually because they have already spied the iconic Woody which ensures instant credibility.

Tom is a natural listener, and since people love to talk about their cars, he is more than happy to give them the opportunity. Just a car guy connecting to another car guy. It's that simple.

If you ever get the chance to tag along with Tom, do it! It's a day you will never forget.

One of the most creative automotive photographers in the business, I've been lucky enough to have produced five books with Michael Alan Ross. Michael is up early, goes to bed late, and seemingly never gets tired.
Michael Alan Ross

I was researching a book on historic Porsche racing cars, and as I scanned scores of sixty- and seventy-year-old race results, I noticed a last name that kept popping up. Actually, two guys with the same last name who raced Porsches and HRGs at races in Florida, at Bridgehampton on Long Island, and some other East Coast tracks during the early 1950s. Their name caught my attention because their listed hometown was very close to where I grew up on Long Island. After seeing that last name in a dozen or more race results, I decided I needed to look these guys up. Not that I suspected they might be still alive—having raced sports cars in the early 1950s would mean they had likely passed—but maybe a relative could tell me more about their racing exploits. Maybe there was still racing memorabilia—trophies and the like—still sitting in a basement. Or better yet, perhaps an old Porsche race car was lurking in the garage. (There goes that darn imagination again . . .)

I called my long-time friend, Bill Etts, who owns a furniture store in the same town. I asked if he knew the family. "No," he said, "but I'll do some snooping."

A day later, Bill called me. "I just spoke to Jay, his son," he said. "He said he can't wait to speak with you. He's waiting for your call."

I called immediately and spoke with Jay. He told me that both his uncle and his father were early road racers, and that he grew up going to the races with them as a child. After a while, I had to ask . . . "Is there any chance one of the old race cars still exists?"

Jay told me, no, they had been sold at least fifty years ago. Oh, too bad, I only missed them by half a century . . .

But then he started to tell me about his own road racing. He had raced a Mustang Shelby GT350 at tracks like Bridgehampton and Lime Rock for years. He had converted it from a street car into a B-Production race car, but hadn't raced it in more than twenty-five years. "I still have it in the garage."

I went silent. I had hoped to find out about his father's and his uncle's old race cars, but it turns out the second-generation racer, Jay, still had his old race car!

This story is not over yet. I've sworn off buying more cars, but a GT350 is another issue. I'll let you know how it turns out.

The lesson here is that there is no idea or method too crazy in the effort to find old cars. If the idea produces positive results, it was a good one. And if it doesn't, it was a bad one. Except sometimes. You see, what doesn't work in one instance may work in the next.

Alway keep your bag of tricks handy.

I truly believe that old cars can be found everywhere.

I am willing to bet that even a metropolis like New York City likely houses many old cars in both public and private garages. This is based on my experience as a kid when my father brought my brother Rob and I to the New York International Auto Show at the Coliseum, probably in 1965 or 1966. I was about twelve-years-old. We parked the family VW in a public parking garage, and because it was crowded, we had to park way down on the lowest level. When we got there, our tiny VW was surrounded by large, prewar classics—Rolls Royces, Pierce-Arrows, who knows what else—that were covered in decades of dust. I surmised that these were owned by wealthy families who lived in the surrounding penthouses. In actuality, these cars were probably all but forgotten and more likely burdens to the owners. I often wonder what happened to those cars and how many more might still be resting in The City That Never Sleeps.

Talking about New York City . . .

One day, Jay Leno called me. I won't say we are best friends, but we have each other's cell phone numbers and we talk and visit occasionally because we share the same automotive interests.

"Hey, Tom, I've got a doozy for you . . . you'll never guess what I found in a Manhattan parking garage," he said.

I couldn't imagine.

"A Duesenberg," he said. It was a prestigious brand of which he already owned several examples. "And it has a great story. Listen to this . . . "

While he was holiday shopping with his wife, Mavis, he decided to follow up on a lead he had heard about, a Duesenberg in a public parking garage near Macy's Department Store in the Herald Square area of Manhattan.

"There are some vehicles—Vincent Motorcycles, Alfa Romeos, some Harley-Davidsons—that have myths that develop around them," he said. "Duesenberg are that type of vehicle."

He didn't know which garage the car might be in, so while Mavis shopped, he walked the neighborhood searching out parking garages and asking the attendants if there were any old cars stored there.

"Sure," they would say, and they would guide him either up to the top floor or down to the basement. "Sometimes, it would be a Rolls Royce; sometimes, it would be a Ford Maverick," he said.

Eventually, he came to a garage at 57th Street and Park Avenue, which is where he laid eyes on the Duesenberg he had heard rumors about.

"It was a 1931 Model J, not the most beautiful or desirable model, but every Duesenberg is special," he said. "The car had six inches of dust around it because nobody had swept the floor there in seventy years. And there was a drip, drip, drip of water from a leaky pipe above the car that, over the decades, had worn a hole through one of the front fenders."

Jay explained the car had accrued parking fees in excess of $80,000 for the wealthy owner who had parked it there in 1933 and forgotten about it.

"Did you buy it," I asked?

"No," he said. "The garage management company had installed new elevators a couple of years earlier and the Duesenberg was just too large to be accommodated in the new, smaller elevators. It will be up there forever, I guess."

Wow, too bad, I thought. Cool story, though.

That conversation took place in about 2001. A decade later, Jay called to tell me that he had purchased the Manhattan Duesey and it just been delivered to his shop in Burbank, California.

"Wait, how did you get the car down without an elevator?" I asked.

"Oh, that was just a story I made up to keep nosey people away until I could complete the purchase of the car. Sorry."

Son of a gun, he was able to purchase a barn find from Midtown Manhattan, literally surrounded by millions of people and probably fifty miles from the nearest barn! All because he bothered to ask someone likely to know, in this case garage attendants, if there were any interesting cars at hand.

If a Duesenberg can hide in the middle of the busiest city in the world, old cars are hiding everywhere.

LOTUS ELAN

My wife Pat and I jumped into the Porsche 356 we owned at the time and drove toward the North Carolina Smokey Mountains to participate in an Austin-Healey convention (our Healey 100-6 was still under restoration and not yet roadworthy). We had a great time driving the twists around Asheville and checking out all the beautiful British cars.

We had overnight accommodations at a nice B & B in Little Switzerland. In the morning, delivered to our bedroom door were coffee, orange juice, two amazing, warm blueberry muffins, and a copy of the Sunday edition of the *Asheville Citizen-Times* newspaper. (Newspapers . . . remember those?)

As we enjoyed our breakfast, I scanned the paper to see what had happened in the world the day before while we had been driving our non-radio equipped car. Then, of course, I checked out the "Automobiles" section, specifically the "Classified Ads" classic car section. (Remember classifieds?)

Of the six or so "antique" cars listed was a Model A Ford, a Lotus Esprit, and a 1967 Lotus Elan Series III coupe. The Elan caught my eye, especially when I read that it had been previously owned by two-time Formula One World Champion Graham Hill. The asking price was $5,000.

"Babe, check this out," I said to Pat. "We're going to take a little drive to check out this car if I can get in touch with the owner."

I called and called and called, but no answer. This was in the 1980s and cell phones and answering machines were luxuries.

Anyway, we continued to have fun driving

through the mountains with the Healey boys before arriving back home Sunday night.

Finally on Monday, I connected with the owner, Chris, who lived in the town of Pisgah in, get this, Transylvania County, North Carolina. He said he had acquired the car many years earlier, purchased from a man who had purchased it from family friend Graham Hill.

I was later able to confirm that both factory F-1 Lotus drivers, Hill and Jimmy Clark, each received new Elan coupes as gifts from Lotus founder Colin Chapman. Hill's was yellow, and so was Chris' car. Or at least it had been yellow, by the time I saw it, it was mostly covered in gray primer.

I made an appointment to visit the car the next day, which was about a two-and-a-half-hour drive from my house near Charlotte Motor Speedway.

The next day, I arrived at Chris' shop by mid-morning. Chris was a cabinet maker, so the car sat in the back of his wood shop literally coated in sawdust. Worse than that, Chris had partially disassembled the car and all the internals were coated in sawdust as well. I'm talking about pistons, connecting rods, crankshaft, and oily nuts and bolts in a bin, all covered in fine wood dust.

The body was only resting on the chassis, and everything else was in a big pile. A mess, but still, it was only $5,000.

That's when he told me his phone had been ringing off the hook over the past two days, and he had a standing offer from a man in Michigan for $10,000.

So, this was going to become a bidding war. Since I didn't know Lotuses, it was difficult for me to do an inventory of the parts, but because

I bought Formula One driver Graham Hill's personal Lotus Elan coupe from a cabinet shop in the North Carolina mountains. Besides being totally covered in sawdust, it was complete but disassembled. How it got there from the United Kingdom is a mystery. *Tom Cotter*

it had been Graham Hill's car, I was glassy eyed. At the time, I followed Formula One and Hill was one of my favorite drivers. I agreed to buy the car for $10,000 and planned to pick it up the following Saturday. We shook hands and I drove back toward Charlotte.

Saturday came and my friend Andy Russell and I drove back to Pisgah with my truck and trailer and loaded it up. Later that day we unloaded the Lotus in my garage . . . where it sat untouched for five years.

Preparing to move to a new home, I decided it was time to sell the Lotus because I had not invested even one hour's work on the car in the five years I had owned it.

I advertised it in *Hemmings Motor News* and sold it for $10,000, exactly what I had paid, to a Lotus enthusiast in England, who was gung-ho to complete the car's restoration.

Last he and I spoke, in 2020, or at least twenty years since I sold the car, it was still sitting in his garage, awaiting restoration . . .

As I related earlier in the book, my next-door neighbor, Hugh Barger, drove an AC Greyhound when he was in graduate school. The car is rare, but not very desirable. Built from 1959 to 1963, only eighty-three examples were constructed. Nearly all the parts on the Greyhounds were proprietary. In the late 1960s or early 1970s, when Hugh's car had a faulty brake master cylinder—and he was unable to locate a replacement or repair kit—he parked the car in his barn.

It's still sitting there today.

The Greyhound is an unusual car and not in great demand. Traditionally, car collectors have been attracted to prestige cars: ones built in small numbers by major manufacturers that were ultra-elegant or had enviable competition histories. Witness the desirability of Ford GTs, Chevy Corvette Grand Sports, Duesenberg, Ferrari GTOs, and so on.

"Off-beat" cars are usually ignored and left for others to discover.

That is, until recently.

In this era, folks are flocking to unusual cars. Notice the attention and relatively high bids that orphan and other less popular cars achieve on bringatrailer.com: the more unique, the better. Simcas, Renaults, VW Beetles, Ramblers, station wagons, pickup trucks, Slant Six Mopars, Alfa Romeo panel deliveries, Hillman Minxes, Morris Minors, Peugeots, Humber Super Snipes, Trabants, all Citroen models—enthusiasts are seeking vehicles that are individual and a one-of-one to drive to a local Cars & Coffee event on Saturday morning.

I enjoy this trend. After all, how many Mustangs and Corvettes can be appreciated at a car show? These red-headed stepchild cars seem to attract

the largest crowds and an unprecedented amount of attention. These cars are finally getting the attention they have been denied for decades while more popular brands stole the spotlight.

The downside with unusual cars relates to parts, maintenance, and repairs. Where will you find the parts? Who is competent to repair them?

When you figure that out, let me know where an AC Greyhound brake master cylinder can be sourced.

9

HOW THE
PROS
DO IT

When friend Ken Gross gifted me a copy of James Melton's *Bright Wheels Rolling*, I realized I was not the first one to write about finding old cars in barns. If you are a barn find geek like me, it's worth searching for a copy on Amazon and giving it a read. *Tom Cotter*

est we think our generation invented the "science" of searching for old cars, I'll let you in on a little secret—we didn't. Forward-thinking collectors actually began hunting for old cars when they were just that, old cars. Henry Austin Clark, Jr., who opened The Long Island Automotive Museum in Southampton in 1948, one of the first antique car museums in the United States, began searching for significant turn-of-the-century cars in the 1930s. Collectors Richard Warth and Tom Barrett traveled the globe, knocking on the doors of castles across Europe and the Middle East offering to take the old Mercedes-Benzes, Bugattis, and Duesenbergs off the hands of kings and noblemen. They did this all without the ability to use the Internet or cell phones.

We have something to learn from these pioneers whose footsteps we now follow. Their seat-of-the-pants methods for unearthing desirable cars can still be applied today even in our seemingly fully connected world.

JAMES MELTON, WORLD-FAMOUS TENOR ON RADIO, TV, AND OPERA—AND WORLD-CLASS CAR COLLECTOR

My good friend Ken Gross, automotive journalist par excellence, my coauthor on *Rockin' Garages*, former director of The Petersen Automotive Museum in Los Angeles, and the former owner of the largest flathead Ford intake manifold collection on earth, called me one day a couple of years ago.

"Tom, do you have a copy of *Bright Wheels Rolling*," he asked.

I had to admit, no, and that I had never heard of it.

"It's a book about finding old cars that was written in the 1950s by James Melton and Ken Purdy. I'll find a copy and send it to you."

I had no idea what Ken was talking about, but I appreciated him keeping me in mind. A few months later a UPS package arrived with a copy of the book and a note from Ken: "Enjoy!"

Bright Wheels Rolling was written the year I was born, 1954, which was also the early days of folks' interest in restoring and collecting old cars. James Melton—a renowned singer I barely knew of—wrote the book with celebrated automotive journalist Ken Purdy.

It turns out Melton was quite an old car enthusiast and had once owned Autorama, a significant antique car collection, first located in Connecticut and then relocated to Florida. The book jacket claimed Autorama was world-famous.

Melton started collecting cars in the 1930s, when antique cars were merely old cars. Thanks to his large fan base, when he asked an owner if he could buy an old car, they had a hard time saying no. It's probably similar to the advantage Jay Leno has when he knocks on a door today to ask about the Duesenberg sitting in a downtown parking garage.

Below, I've excerpted some of the passages from Melton's book that relate to discovering and obtaining cars. He begins by stating a collector's resolve for the task ahead: "He will find himself a car if it's the last thing he ever does. How? Well, there are lots of ways." Melton then goes on to cite examples to his approach.

- "He can just go looking. This used to be a sensible method of operation. A man could drive out into the country almost anywhere in the 1930s and be sure that a few dozen inquiries at filling stations, garages, general stores and the like would turn up the name and address of some worthy citizen who had an old car on his hands and wanted to get rid of it. Sometimes you could even get **paid** for hauling the thing away. At any rate, you could be sure of an attractive price. I know a man who, in 1934, paid $50 for a Mercer Runabout, one of the rarest American cars. Ten years later he sold it, paintless and almost bodiless, for a $1,200 profit. Restored it went for $4,500.
- "The method still works—but not very well. The bushes have been well beaten during the last couple of decades. There's too much ground to cover now to be able to do it afoot or on horseback.
- "You can do it by mail. I know a man who wrote to twelve hundred postmasters in New England asking for leads on old cars and enclosing self-addressed postcards. He didn't do badly.
- "Some newspapers, notably the Sunday edition of *New York Times*, carry classified advertisements offering old cars for sale. Most of them, though, are expensive because they've already been restored. Magazines like *Motor Trend*, *Road and Track*, *Motorsport*, and *Car Life* often have very good leads."

I was amazed by some of the similarities between Melton's approaches and my own.

Melton then gives a hypothetical example of said collector who finds an old car:

"Let's assume that our man finds a worthwhile automobile in reasonable condition for not too much money. Let us say he finds a 1927 Rolls Royce limousine in pretty rough shape as far as bodywork is concerned, but with a fair engine and a good chassis. He should be able to buy the car for around $400."

This passage is interesting as it shows how the cost of cars has risen with, or faster than, the rate of inflation.

Melton's book goes on to describe some of the more notable cars in his collection, some manufacturers' histories, how he acquired each car, and how much he paid. More than a few were given to him by widows who still had their husband's old car in the garage and wanted a good home for it. Other people would give him their old car in exchange for concert tickets. In any event, Melton had a distinct advantage over other collectors in his era and he used that advantage to the fullest.

My point here is not that you should hope to become a world-famous singer, like Melton, or a renowned comedian, like Leno, to improve your car collecting opportunities. The point is that these guys often work the same angles as the rest of us to make their discoveries.

Collectors of all stripes have equal opportunities to romance long-time owners out of their vehicles. The secret is to sell yourself as being an authentic old car enthusiast, one who will be a worthy custodian for the foreseeable future. If you can envision the negotiation as an adoption rather than an acquisition, it will often put you into the right frame of mind.

TOM SHAUGHNESSY, FERRARI BARN FIND MASTER

"Reward people. Don't negotiate the shit out of them. Make the buyer feel good about selling you the car."

Those are words of advice from Tom Shaughnessy, one of the most prolific car hunters in the business. Tom came into my radar when word got out that he had purchased critical parts for a rare Ferrari race car from an eBay listing. I detailed the story in my 2007 book, *The Hemi in the Barn*, but in a nutshell: Shaughnessy was scanning eBay when he happened upon a fiberglass-bodied Devin sports car. The seller's original intention had been to install a supercharged V-8 engine for drag racing, but he never got around to the conversion, so the car sat.

When Shaughnessy saw the ad, features such as the wire wheels, chassis, suspension, and a serial number instantly jumped out at him. He suspected it was a Ferrari. As it turned out, it was a 1952 340 America with Le Mans racing history. Shaughnessy won the auction, paying $26,912, but he was prepared to spend ten times that much.

Since that eBay buy, he has scored dozens of cars including Ford GT40 P/1067, a Ferrari Series 1 Cabriolet, and a Kurtis Sport Car that was sitting in the high desert.

"Surround yourself with good people and don't be stingy," he preaches. "I share my success because it's not all about me. I don't lowball but pay fair prices with the hope the seller might offer me another car in the future. Or, refer me to his friends."

Shaughnessy started out selling car parts—specifically rare Ferrari parts—and eventually moved to entire cars. "I've built relationships by buying a guy's parts. Eventually, that leads to me buying a car those parts came off. I prefer to deal with the mechanics, not the owners, because I'll eventually get introduced to the owner as a familiar name and a trusted friend of the mechanic.

"The hard stuff to find are the quality pieces that sit in holes and are unseen for years. These are the cars I need leads to find. I'll take leads from anywhere and gladly pay finder's fees."

Shaughnessy cautions would-be classic car owners or restorers: "The new parts you buy these days for old cars are pretty much junk. They may look right, but they are often untested and fail instantly.

"Because quality parts sources are drying up and owners are 'timing out,' good cars are coming back on the market."

RICHIE CLYNE, FORMER PRINCIPAL
OF THE IMPERIAL PALACE AUTO COLLECTION

"I don't search much for cars these days, but when I did, I scoured every old magazine I could. If I was interested in a car that was featured in a magazine years ago, I would try to contact the owner, who would sometimes be deceased. In that case, I could sometimes buy the car that was still in the garage from the widow."

"THE TRANS-AM HUNTER" BY PAT RYAN

Pat Ryan's saga illustrates the lengths to which the most intrepid barn finders will go to uncover a special car once it is on their radar.

My search for a specific car, the very first Penske/Donohue Sunoco Camaro, lasted twenty-five years. In 1989, I bought the second Sunoco Camaro and I am still vintage racing it. I researched its history and met team members and other Sunoco Camaro owners. Six were built, two each year in 1967, 1968, and 1969. Mark Donohue's book *The Unfair Advantage* documents that [the car builds] and was a valuable resource for me.

"Four were vintage racing in the early 1990s. Two were missing. I began my search for the other two. The fifth car, the first 1969, turned out to have been crushed in the 1987 Mexico City earthquake. So, my search narrowed to the first cars.

After chasing a 1967 Z/28 Penske Trans Am Camaro—with its Penske racing parts removed—for a book *Camaro: Untold Secrets/1967–1969*, I learned it had been crushed, and I thought the search had ended. Shortly after learning that information, I met members of the original Penske Team and they told me the 1967 car went with one of their crew members, Peter Rinehart, to race in Germany and Austria. After many years of Internet searching, I found pictures of a car with windshield retaining clips in the same location as the early Donohue pictures. I knew that driver Helmut Marko had raced it for the same team in 1969. More pictures indicated it had then gone to Franz Albert who also raced it in Austria.

I lost the trail because Rinehart disappears in 1985 after a career as a team manager in F1, and Albert had died long ago and his employees did not remember what happened to the car.

After years of chasing clues, I found an anonymous blogger who said he had once had the opportunity to buy the Franz Albert Camaro. It took more years to figure out who it was on that blog who had only signed off as "Jackie." I finally found him, and he knew who had bought it in 1980— a famous Austrian rally driver. It took several more months to get this very wealthy man to respond and to find out if he knew where the next owner might be. He said, "It's in my garage in Austria, taken all apart for a restoration I started in 1981 and abandoned." I asked him to take a picture of the serial number and email it. Another year was lost because he now lived in Spain and the car was still in Austria.

Vintage racer and collector Pat Ryan spent decades searching for Penske Racing's first 1967 Camaro Z/28. It's pictured here with Mark Donohue behind the wheel and Roger Penske assisting in the pit stop. [Revs Institute]

SHELBY GT500

For years, I had heard that Bob Ramsuer had an old Shelby Mustang, but that he was definitely not interested in selling. I had become friendly with Bob while I worked at Charlotte Motor Speedway as Bob's son Stuart raced in the Sportsman series, a low-cost version of NASCAR Cup cars. I found out that decades earlier that Bob had road raced a 1966 Shelby, so we enjoyed talking about racing in the old days at tracks like Virginia International Raceway, Marlboro, and the like.

Bob had sold his race car years earlier, but he still owned a 1967 Shelby GT500 that had been driven by his wife. Every time I asked him about the car, Bob reinforced, "It's not for sale."

I decided to change his mind. At that time, Bob owned a small cafe in the village square in the North Carolina town of Lincolnton, about forty-five minutes from my home. I decided to get up early, drive there, and have breakfast. The pancakes were excellent. As much as I enjoyed sitting at the counter having breakfast, Bob enjoyed having a "newcomer" with whom he could talk road racing in this heart of NASCAR country.

A few weeks later, I returned for lunch. Bob also made a heck of a hamburger. This time, I brought along a gift for Bob, a copy of the book I had written years earlier about the Holman-Moody race team. I signed the book in front of Bob and presented it to him. He was taken aback.

"Tom, you've always been interested in that Shelby I've got," he said. "How would you like to see it?" He said if I could wait a little while so he could clean up the kitchen, we could take a look.

When he was finished, I followed him just a few blocks away to a rental house he kept. There, at the end of the driveway, was a Shelby wearing much patina. It was a big-block 428 Cobra Jet, automatic, and had the later "wide" headlights in the grill.

"I didn't buy it new, but I bought it when it was one year old," Bob explained. "It was my wife's daily driver, although I flat-towed my race car with it to the track a few times. When she started selling real estate, this was not a good car to transport clients with, so we bought her a mini-van and parked this. It hasn't been driven since."

This car was a time capsule: only 34,000 miles and never restored. It even had the original exhaust system, heater and radiator hoses, and distributor points. It even had all those rare little tags that the factory hung from the distributor and carburetor that are often lost over the years.

And it had the item that most Shelby enthusiasts always point out: the little decal applied to the bottom of the hood by the Canadian Allied Fiberglass company that manufactured the hoods for Shelby American.

I invited my good friend Jim Maxwell over to look at the car. We had purchased a couple of Shelbys together over the years. He liked it, so we made Bob a fair offer, market value, and he agreed. We owned the Shelby.

Two days later, I received a call from a local Shelby collector and dealer: "I heard you bought a car I've been chasing for twenty years. How did you do it?"

By frequenting Bob Ramsuer's business and not being aggressive, my friend Jim Maxwell and I were successful in purchasing the Shelby GT500 he had owned since 1968. Because it had never been restored, show judges loved it when we brought it to Shelby meets, using it as a reference for restored cars. *Jim Maxwell*

I explained that I didn't just swoop in to buy the car for a low price, but instead befriended Bob, gave him a gift, and enjoyed his company before discussing the purchase.

Jim and I owned the car for at least a decade, and it became one of the most popular cars at Shelby American Automobile Club (SAAC) meets because of its originality. We finally sold the GT500 in 2020 after having lots of fun with it for years.

The lesson? You must sell yourself before you can buy a car.

After hunting for thirty years, the rare Camaro racer didn't look quite as pretty as it once did, but the serial numbers matched a secret inventory of the first twenty-five Trans-Am Z/28s that were produced by Chevrolet. Many years of restoration of this bare shell resulted in a trophy at the 2020 Amelia Island Concours d'Elegance. *Jon Mello*

Once I got the picture, I could only read four digits of the six. My friend, a Camaro historian, knew the number from Chevrolet records, but I did not have that information. I gave him the picture, and he confirmed that the four numbers matched. I said, "I am going tomorrow to buy the car, and I will send you the other two numbers when I can read them." He asked to come along, so we both went to Austria and he verified the numbers. There were a dozen more specific Penske-fabricated pieces that were still with the car that matched our pictures from the '67 Trans Am races. There was blue and yellow overspray in lots of places. No doubt we found the car. It was all there but totally apart.

It took a week to find a company that could crate the pieces and palletize the body shell and another month to get it home. It took a further three years to put it back together and six months for Kevin Mackay at Corvette Repair in Valley Stream, New York, to make it one hundred-point pretty just in time to debut at the Roger Penske display at the Amelia Island Concours d'Elegance at Amelia Island in March 2020. All five surviving Sunoco Camaros were together there for the first time, and it won the Amelia Award. Roger saw it for the first time in fifty-two years, just like it was when it left his shop (but prettier).

"There were lots more twists and turns to this story, but the upshot is I now have two of the five Penske Trans Am Camaros. Ah, but which one to sell and which one to keep?"

"THEY FIND ME!" BY BILL WARNER, FOUNDER OF THE AMELIA ISLAND CONCOURS D'ELEGANCE

For years, I made my living as a traveling salesman, visiting accounts in Southeast states, hoping they would buy my wares. As a traveling salesman, you have two choices to make during the off hours in strange cities along the way: 1) You can end up in a bar drinking every evening and eventually become an alcoholic . . . or even worse than that; 2) You can scavenge junkyards and repair shops looking for old cars.

I have been luckier than most and have stumbled across a number of really neat cars that I have restored. It's been my life, but it's not like I'm actually hunting for them. They find me!

I was at a magazine stand in Columbia, South Carolina, looking at an issue of *Road & Track* when an enthusiast next to me mentioned that there was an old race car in Broom's Junkyard just a few miles away. I drove there and Bill Broom showed me a 1964 Brabham BT8 Sports Racer. He got it as a trade for a VW Beetle and an old pickup truck. The Brabham was powered by a 2-liter Coventry Climax engine and originally driven by Denny Hulme.

Following up on a lead, Bill Warner discovered and purchased this Braham BT8 from a Columbia, South Carolina, junkyard. Originally raced by driver Denny Hulme, the car had extensive racing history in Europe and South Africa. Bill paid $2,900 for the Brabham, restored it, and said it was one of the best cars he has ever raced. *Bill Warner*

Following up on a lead, Bill Warner found the Lang Cooper, known as the King Cobra when it was campaigned by Carroll Shelby. Warner bought, restored, and raced it, but he sold it when he found it unwieldy to drive. Asking former team drivers, they all agreed the car was basically undrivable. *Bill Warner*

I bought it for $2,900. Only twelve were built, and it had been raced by Hulme all over Europe and South Africa. That was one of the best race cars I've ever driven.

One year later, Broom called me and said he had a Lang Cooper Ford race car, one of only eight built by Carroll Shelby as the King Cobra. My friend, photographer Dave Freidman, gave me photos of the car being built in the Shelby shops and racing at Riverside and Laguna Seca. I bought that one as well.

The only car I really chased was the Edsel Ford Speedster, and I chased it not to own it, but to convince the owner to display it at Amelia Island. I had heard rumors that the car was hiding somewhere in Central Florida. I tracked it down in Deland, Florida, just an hour from where I live in Jacksonville. It was covered with a bunch of stuff in the owner's carport. I consider it my greatest find.

The Group 44 Triumph TR6 fell into my lap when the owner was sitting next to me on pit wall at Watkins Glen. He said, "You just need to buy my Triumph race car from me," so I did for $12,000. It had a great history where Bob Tullius, John McComb, and then Paul Newman won National Championships in the car. I restored it and had fun racing it for twenty-eight years.

Here are some of my rules for finding cars, even though the Internet has screwed it all up:

- Get excited about your finds! For the right car, I still get as excited as a kid.
- Work your contacts.
- The fun is finding a sow's ear and making it into a silk purse.
- You have to keep your antenna up and follow every rumor.
- I believe more old cars will begin coming to market as this generation of owners age and die.
- Research the car before you buy it. Don't take anyone's word; find out the real story. I truly love hearing the story.
- I don't like to invest in cars where more than 1,000 were built.
- Don't try to buy it for the lowest price. I still kick myself for the RS60 Porsche Spyder I lost because I would not increase my offer by just $1,000.
- Never borrow money for a collector car. It's just too risky.

In a case of *fact being stranger than fiction*, photographer Dave Friedman provided Warner with an image of his two cars in the same race: the 1964 Los Angeles Times Grand Prix at Riverside Raceway, turn 9. The King Cobra is on the left, and the Brabham is on the right. How they both ended up in the same South Carolina junkyard is anybody's guess. *Dave Friedman*

Tom Miller reluctantly followed up a lead his father gave him about a Mercedes hardtop in the classified ad section of a daily newspaper. Like a dream, it turned out to be a Gullwing. He bought it, but only owned it a short time. *Tom Miller*

"SOMETIMES A MERCEDES IS ACTUALLY A GULLWING" BY TOM MILLER, OWNER OF TOM MILLER SPORTS AND CLASSIC CARS

"I got into buying and selling cars back in 1987. It began with the Jaguar XK140 I found on the side of the road. I sold it to a Dutch guy, which began a partnership between the two of us. I sent more than 500 cars from the United States to Europe. This was just a part-time gig because I owned a printing company at the time.

"Since selling the printing business in 2007, I've been at it full-time. Now, I partner with a guy from Austria, and we've sold more than 900 cars, mostly to Europe.

"Once, my father called me. He had seen a Mercedes-Benz 300SL Hardtop [Gullwing] in the newspaper in 2008. I said, 'Dad, it can't be.' But when I called, it was actually a Gullwing. At the time, I was financially tapped out because of my business. So, I partnered with another old car dealer, each of us owning fifty percent.

"When I am on vacation, I'm checking the papers. I used to buy on eBay a lot. Sometimes, I have to buy two cars in order to get the car I really want. Those can be difficult deals.

"When I go to car shows, I always strike up conversations. I keep notebooks that I never throw away. They are filled with people's names and the cars they own. At Hershey, I always hear about cars that I follow up later."

"EARS WIDE OPEN" BY MATT DEGARMO, FOUNDER OF DEGARMO LTD.

I'm not a barn finder in the true sense of the word. I don't find cars as much as they find me. For instance, I sold a Jaguar E-Type to a gentleman in Toronto. Sometime after he bought the car, he called and told me he had overheard a woman at a cocktail party. She said her deceased husband's Porsche 356 was sitting in the garage at their San Francisco home, and she didn't know what to do with it.

I was put in touch with this woman, and even though she was a bit strange, I stayed in touch with her for two years and wound up buying the car, a 1959 Convertible D. It turns out her husband was an American fighter pilot and had bought the car new from a Porsche dealership in Tokyo, Japan. It was amazingly documented; her husband saved every single piece of paper related to the purchase and ownership of the car.

I started my business about thirty-five years ago by importing right-hand drive Bentley Saloons from England. I didn't even know if there was a market for them in the States, but the dollar exchange rate was excellent, and I would have considered it a fun adventure even if the idea had failed.

"The Bentley sedans led to a Bentley R-Type Continental Fastback—left-hand drive, 4.9-liter, four-speed manual gearbox—which is a very desirable car. I bought that from a man whose grandfather had died and left him a Rolls Royce and the Bentley. He had the Bentley appraised by someone who

Matt DeGarmo was importing relatively inexpensive Bentley sedans from the United Kingdom and selling them in the United States when he stumbled upon a very desirable Continental coupe in Milwaukee. With left-hand drive and a four-speed gearbox, he rushed to buy it and getting it on a transporter ASAP, not wanting to be part of a bidding war. *Matt DeGarmo*

Having started barn find hunting in the 1980s, Matt DeGarmo said he was able to discover cars like this Jaguar XK coupe much easier than he can today. *Matt DeGarmo*

didn't know what he was doing who gave a value that was too low. I told him that the car was worth way more than the appraisal, which probably endeared him to me for being honest.

His grandfather had owned the car since 1960, but it had been off the road for years and needed lots of work to make it roadworthy. I flew to Milwaukee and arranged to have a flatbed truck hide around the corner. As soon as I secured the car, I had it loaded up and taken away. I didn't want anybody else showing up to start a bidding war.

On his way into the operating room, MG enthusiast Tony Giordano got a call on his cell phone from the lady he had been trying to contact to buy her late husband's MG TC! After surgery, he closed the deal. Who says barn find hunters can take a day off? *Tony Giordano*

It all comes down to listening very carefully and never giving up. My overhead is low because I work out of my house. My father was in advertising and he was ruthless; once he got his mind set on securing a new account, he didn't let up until he had them as a client. I guess I learned my business ethics from my dad, although I'm not quite as aggressive as he was."

"THE SHARK THAT NEVER SLEEPS" BY TIM SUDDARD, PUBLISHER OF *CLASSIC MOTORSPORT* AND *GRASSROOTS MOTORSPORT* MAGAZINES

In my business of restoring old cars and writing about it, I am offered more cars than I can use. I still enjoy the hunt, so even though I receive lots of leads from readers, I really enjoy finding cars on my own.

I think the real hunter is like a shark that never sleeps. I never read anything without looking at the classifieds in the back. I always take the back roads when I can. If I drive up a rural road in one direction one day, I will always come back in the other direction another day.

The biggest thing is you constantly need to be looking. You make your own luck. If you are looking for something specific, like a 1965 Corvette, now that's hard. But if you like everything, you can't fail.

If a friend calls to tell me he's going to look at an old car, and do I want to come along, I'll always say yes, because I'm not interested in the car my friend is looking at, but potentially the car parked behind that—or the one behind that. A buddy of mine was going to look at a Jaguar E-Type and asked if I wanted to go. Then, he said, 'Oh, there's supposed to be an old Triumph race car in the garage as well.' So we went there, and the Triumph turns out to be a TR3 that raced in the Daytona 24 Hours twice! It was stuffed into the garage after it last raced in 1965 and covered with old Daytona 24 Hour posters. So, my buddy did not buy the Jag, but I bought the Triumph.

When I travel to make sales calls for the magazines, I visit a lot of shops. I always check out what's parked out back. I'm not as interested in the pretty cars in the showroom or in the shop.

When I go for a bicycle ride with Margie, my wife, she does it for the exercise, but I go to look for old cars in the neighborhoods."

TONY GIORDANO, THE MGC GOD

Tony Giordano has a day job: he's an Investment Advisor. He steers millions of dollars into investments for his well-heeled clients. He's also a part-time drummer in a band that occasionally includes some of the original Blue Oyster Cult members. But whether he's searching for investments or banging out the rhythm for "Godzilla," he's always thinking about his next old car discovery.

Giordano is a British car enthusiast, and MGs are his true passion. But of all MGs, his favorite car is the unusual and rare MGC, a six-cylinder-powered MGB. He told me a story about getting a call at 2 a.m. while he and his wife were sleeping. His wife answered the phone, and the caller asked for "the MGC God." It was a call from a fellow enthusiast in Belgium.

Giordano works the MG crowd around the world for new leads.

"My father bought me my first MGB when I went off to college, a beautiful British Racing Green 1971," he recalled. "But eventually I fell in love with the MGC because I couldn't afford a $70,000 Austin Healey, but I could afford a $5,000 MGC. And, I could build a hot engine and have something almost as good as a Healey."

Giordano told me that of the 9,000 MGCs produced, he figures he has owned approximately 10 percent of them.

How does he do it?

For one thing, instead of buying any car that he finds, he ONLY buys MGs: MGB, MGCs, and MGT-series cars.

"I join all the clubs and have friends all over the country, actually all over the world," he says. "I get all the newsletters and subscribe to all the online message boards. I know exactly who has what."

Because he has so many friends, he is constantly getting emails and phone calls with leads for newly discovered cars. But sometimes, these calls come at the most inopportune times . . .

He had been following up a lead on an MG TC. It was owned by a woman who lived in Bucks County, in Pennsylvania, whose husband had died, and she needed to dispose of his cars. Giordano had tried to get in touch with her without success.

"Well, I was lying on a hospital gurney literally being wheeled into the operating room to have stents put in my heart when the phone rang," he said. "This woman was finally returning my calls. And I was going into surgery in like ten minutes. We spoke for a few minutes, and I told her I'd have to call her back because I was being wheeled into heart surgery. We became friends, and I ultimately bought the TC from her."

Sticking to one brand has its benefits. Few people know as much as Giordano does about MGs in general and MGCs in particular. He networks with other enthusiasts and is often the first call when a desirable car surfaces. He doesn't deal in million dollar cars, but he deals in cars that everybody can afford.

He might just be onto something there.

"SEEK AND YE SHALL FIND" BY DAVE HINTON, PRESIDENT OF HISTORIC SPORTSCAR RACING (HSR) AND OWNER OF HERITAGE MOTORSPORTS, INC.

I ran the Le Mans Classic a few years ago in a friend's car and decided I needed to find my own old Jag with International Race History to race there myself. I started to go through old magazines and race results from 1961 through about 1970 and tracing chassis numbers. There was a Series 1 coupe that kept coming up, both in race results and websites. These days, you can do a pretty good job searching for old cars from your desk at home. The

Giordano's bread-and-butter is the MGC, a six-cylinder variant of the popular MGB that gave Austin Healey–like performance for half the price. Giordano found this one on Long Island, not far from his house on the South Shore. *Tony Giordano*

(OVERLEAF) Sometimes, Tim Suddard drags home Triumph TR3s, and sometimes, he drags home the worst Lotus Elan on the planet. This car, discovered in Traverse City, Michigan, along with the Lotus Cortina, were purchased and brought back to his home in Florida. The Cortina was sold, but the Elan was restored to Concours condition! *Tim Suddard*

car had quite a racing history, having raced four times each at Daytona and Sebring. It was just what I was looking for.

Anyway, the driver of this 1961 Jag coupe was Richard Robson, but all the early photos were credited to a Guy Anderson, so I started searching for his name. I found Guy on an MG Midget chat page, which I had to join in order to communicate with him.

"I see that your name is attached to a number of photographs of a certain Jag race car," I wrote in an e-mail. "Can you tell me something about the car?"

"Well, I should [be able to]. I own the car," replied Anderson.

Richard told me he lived in Woodstock, Georgia, and would be glad to meet me at Road Atlanta in a couple of weeks when I was racing there. We met, but he told me he didn't want to sell the Jaguar, that he was in the process of restoring the car. He did invite me to see the car any time I was near Woodstock, though. He'd call on occasion and ask what kind of torsion bars he should buy and such, and I'd recommend a brand. Our conversations went on for about a year, when one day I received a phone call from a mutual friend. He told me Guy had just died of a massive heart attack, and the family wanted to sell the car.

I sent a deposit, having never actually seen the car. Soon after someone else came along and offered more money than I had, but Guy's two daughters respected my deposit. Guy had also owned an interesting H-Modified car, which Ray Evernham bought, and a couple of Panteras.

After I owned it, I researched its history further through the paperwork I had acquired. Guy bought the car in about 2000 or 2001. The coupe, which was the 94th left-hand drive E-Type coupe built, was delivered new to Jacksonville, Florida. The second owner, Richard Robson, bought it in 1964 and raced it in the 1964 Daytona Continental, where he DNF'd (did not finish). He raced it at Daytona and Sebring from 1964 until 1969, when he parked it in his garage after blowing the engine at Daytona.

I bought the Jag and restored it, but sadly, I sold it to someone who wanted it more than I did. During this pandemic, my businesses are hurting, so I couldn't afford to keep it.

My second racing Jag discovery was referred to me by my friend Bill Terry, owner of TT Race Engines, and the original sponsor of my Green Card when I emigrated from the UK to live and work in the United States.

Bill called me one day and said, "Hey, you like early E-Types with race history. I just built an engine for an early E-Type, the 75th left-hand drive Roadster."

Bill told me the car had raced in a number of events throughout the United States, including Nassau Speed Weeks, which were the international credentials I sought. From the SCCA logbook, I was able to see every race the car had run from 1964 through 1966.

The original owner was from Oklahoma. I started to do additional research to learn who else had driven it. That owner sold it to a man in Chicago who raced it in the Midwest until he moved to California, where it

Jaguar racer and restorer David Hinton has discovered a number of authentic Jaguar race cars by searching through old SCCA archives. This is one E-type coupe that is just returning from the sandblaster. *David Hinton*

raced at Riverside. It was then sold to a racer in Pennsylvania, who raced it, but mostly hill climbed it. It was then sold to another owner in Illinois, who sold it to the man I bought it from.

When I did additional research, I found the car no longer had its original engine and had a reproduction serial number plate. This is never good when buying a vintage racer because it becomes difficult to verify its authenticity.

It gets complicated here. The second to last owner before me, Steve Cantrell, had a business parting out old Jag E-Types and selling parts. A friend of mine who restores Jags in Maryland told me he had just bought out the parts inventory from Steve Cantrell. Included in the pile of parts were the original cylinder heads from the E-Type I had just bought, in addition to the original number plate!

I bought the car, but I was badgered to death by buyers in England who wanted the car, so regretfully, I sold it.

The moral of the story is They Are Still Out There! It takes persistence. A generation of enthusiasts who own the cars we love are dying off, and the cars are making their way back into the market. The number of people exiting this hobby far, far exceeds the number of new enthusiasts entering it.

You must talk to people all the time. The cars I own attract attention at the events I attend. They often invite conversations that begin with, "You know, I have a neighbor who has a car just like that in his garage."

I'll tape a sign to the windshield of one of the old Jags I drive to the track: "Wanted Old Jags." I'll usually get a couple of leads every weekend.

I'm chasing down one more Jag in Florida, probably the last early race car in existence. In the meantime, I just bought an old Falcon Sprint that I plan to convert into a vintage race car and have some fun again.

KEVIN MACKAY, *THE CORVETTE HUNTER*

When Kevin Mackay, then twenty-eight-years-old, opened a Corvette specialty shop in Valley Stream, Long Island, he never imagined that thirty-six years later he'd be considered the world authority on vintage Corvettes and Corvette race cars. He has recently published his own book, *The Corvette Hunter*, because he has also become an authority in tracking down old Corvette race cars.

"I used to go through old car magazines," recalled the now sixty-four-year-old Mackay. "When I found an article written about a famous Corvette race car, I would try to find the owner's or a mechanic's name. I started doing this in the 1980s, so a lot of those guys were still around then. If they were alive, I contacted them. If not, I tried to contact their wife, son, or daughter."

One car Mackay tried to find was a rather audacious 1966 Corvette drag car called *The Old Reliable*. His search proves that not all barn find stories have happy endings.

"It was ugly, but kind of cool," he said. "It was identifiable because the nose had been extended and had six side slots where a stock '66 only had three."

The original owner had died, so Mackay spoke with one of the mechanics who used to work on the car. Kevin asked where the car might be found today?

"I know exactly what happened to that car," the mechanic said. "It was so ugly we couldn't sell it, so we had a party one night at the shop and lit it on fire. We cooked hot dogs and toasted marshmallows in that blaze. That car will never be found because it doesn't exist."

One of the race cars Mackay had sought for decades was the #1 Corvette that raced at Le Mans in 1960 as part of the three-car Briggs Cunningham effort. The car, which had been driven by Cunningham and Bill Kimberly, crashed early and was a DNF after just thirty-two laps. The car had not been seen in public in decades.

The #2 car, driven by Dick Thompson and Fred Windridge, was also a DNF after 207 laps, but the #3 car, driven by John Fitch and Bob Grossman, finished eighth overall and first in the GT class. Both of those cars are well documented, restored, and sit in private collections.

BARN FIND HUNTER
REDUX

by Brian Cotter

The third-generation "FD" Mazda RX-7 has always been a dream car for me. From an early age, I remember lusting after this unique sports car while playing *Gran Turismo* with friends. When I was bored, I would search Craigslist, eBay, and local classifieds for my dream RX-7, but finding one that had not been modified beyond recognition was near impossible.

As I approached driving age, my search for an RX-7 intensified, but my parents would (wisely) not budge despite my insistence that the twin-turbo sports car would make a perfect first car. Reluctantly, I gave up searching.

Some time later, my dad met a man who lived just around the corner from us, a farmer, who was a car-guy. He invited my dad over to see the interesting cars that resided on his property which included an AC Greyhound, an Alfa Romeo GTV, and in the basement of his farmhouse, a 1993 Mazda RX-7. As it turned out, the silver-over-red RX-7 was purchased new in 1993 under unique circumstances. After reading about the RX-7 in many automotive magazines, the farmer went to his local Mazda dealer (Mazda of Concord, North Carolina) and requested an extended test drive. After writing two checks to the dealer, one for the MSRP for the car, the other for a couple thousand dollars, he set off for a "test drive" to Florida. It was agreed with the sales staff at the dealership that if he liked the car, he would buy it upon his return and the smaller check would be voided; if he didn't love the car, the dealer would be able to cash the smaller check and void the large check.

He loved the car and elected to buy it at the end of his 1,500-mile test drive. Over the next fifteen or so years the car was used sparingly, accumulating about 40,000 miles before being mothballed in the basement of his farmhouse.

When my dad mentioned that my dream car was sitting less than a mile from my home, unused, I was intrigued. After visiting the car a few times, taking plenty of photos, and doing a significant amount of research, I made an offer for the car, which was accepted.

Today, I autocross the RX-7 in the Atlanta, Georgia, area, but have kept it as stock as possible. It frequently attracts passionate rotary fans at local Cars & Coffee events, and I am happy to share the car's story with anyone who will listen.

Just a half-mile from where Brian Cotter grew up sat this Mazda RX-7 in the basement of a farmhouse. Because it had sat for so long, he was able to buy it from the original owner at a reasonable price. The car turned out to be mechanically sound and is now regularly used as a daily driver and an autocross car. *Jordan Lewis*

Master Corvette restorer, Kevin Mackay, had been chasing the number 1 1960 Briggs Cunningham Corvette for decades. Here it is before the start of the 1960 24 Hours of Le Mans beside the two other team cars. *Revs Institute, Inc.*

Not knowing where to start with hunting down the #1 Corvette, though, Mackay talked with Ed Mueller, who owned the only 1967 Corvette to have competed at Le Mans. Mueller gave MacKay a big clue: Le Mans organizers had the vehicle identification numbers (VINs) for every car that has ever competed on the circuit. MacKay felt that if he could obtain the serial number for the #1 car, he at least had a chance of either finding the car or discovering its fate.

"I wrote a nice letter to the folks at Le Mans and a year later I still had no answer," he said. "Of course, I wrote it in English because I don't know French. So, I approached a French school near me to see if they would translate my letter to French, which they did. The school also suggested I send a bouquet of flowers with the letter because the ladies in the Le Mans office might respond more favorably to that."

Mackay had his letter delivered with flowers and three months later he received a response that listed the VINs for all three Cunningham Corvettes. Score!

With the VIN in hand, Mackay got in touch with a New York City police lieutenant friend who did a stolen vehicle search. The search led to an outdated address on Delaware Street in Tampa, Florida. Mackay visited the city, knocked on doors, asked local Corvette owners, but no luck. He even hired a psychic to visit the neighborhood and see if any of the garage doors emitted "good vibrations."

"After nineteen years of searching for that car, it finally found me," he said.

It turns out the car had been stored for decades in a Tampa, Florida, warehouse, near where Mckay had spent years searching.

After its short racing career at Le Mans, the #1 car was sold retail to someone who customized it with single headlights, Burgundy paint, radiused rear fenders, and a Fiat-looking grill. In 1976, it was purchased by a judge for just $200.

"This judge was a hoarder," said Mackay. "It was jammed into a warehouse surrounded by dozens of other cars, bicycles, baby carriages, just junk."

And nobody had a clue that it was actually one of the rarest Corvettes and desired by collectors around the world.

Eventually, the hoarding judge died and his son wanted to sell the car. Because he couldn't locate the car's serial number in the door jamb, its usual location, he lifted the body off the frame to locate the chassis number stamped on the frame. He Googled that number and realized his dad's Corvette had actually been a race car, which led him to contacting the Briggs Cunningham website, operated by Larry Berman in Boston.

"There's a guy in Tampa who claims he owns the Cunningham #1 Corvette," Berman told Mackay.

"Within a second of seeing the photo, I knew it was the car because of the odd location of the hole for windshield wiper," said Mackay.

A deal was negotiated, and Mackay was finally able to own the car of his dreams for $75,000.

Everyone was happy. Well, that was until multiple lawsuits kicked in, but that's an entirely different story, better told on another day.

CUNNINGHAM
BARN FINDS

by Chuck Schoendorf

In the early 1950's, famed American racer Briggs S. Cunningham built a total of thirty-six Cunningham cars, eight of them pure race cars and twenty-eight road-going GT cars. That was the entire run. Of the thirty-six, one race car was scrapped, but miraculously all the GT cars remain. Among the GT cars, three were built, bodied, and completed at the B. S. Cunningham Company shop in West Palm Beach, Florida. The other twenty-five street cars, known as the C-3 or the Continental, had their chassis built at Cunningham's Florida shop and then shipped by boat to Italy to be bodied and completed at the Vignale shop in Torino. Upon completion, they were sent back to the states and sold. The result was a highly stylish, powerful, and expensive GT car.

It was at the first Cunningham Gathering in January 2011, at Mar-a-Lago of all places, that I met Tom Cotter. Tom showed up with his pretty much as-found C-3 coupe No. 5207, and I was there with my freshly restored C-3 coupe No. 5214, which I bought completely disassembled and missing many pieces in 2006. But that's another story.

Eleven of the twenty-five Vignale bodied C-3s showed up in 2011, but what had become of the other fourteen? We knew where several of them were but what about the rest? Thanks to a comprehensive *Cunningham Car Register* compiled in 1982 by then C-3 owner B. Bruce Briggs, we had some leads, but twenty-nine years had elapsed since that was published. Perusing a list of the missing cars, B. Bruce Briggs cited car No. 5209 as being owned by a Harry Sefried in Connecticut. I live in Connecticut, and it's a fairly small state, so I volunteered to see what I

could find out about it. A quick Internet search produced a six-year-old obituary for Harry, but did he own the car when he died? And what did his heirs know, if anything?

Turns out not only did Harry still have the car at his death but his daughter, Leslie, still owned Harry's house on the Connecticut coast in Madison. Leslie told me her father's C-3 was behind the house, right where Harry parked it years or decades earlier.

That was the good news. The bad news was the car was not in the dry barn 200 feet away, but outdoors. In the dirt. Under a blue plastic tarp. Below a grove of shade trees. I'm sure the tarp seemed like a good idea at the time to keep water out, but the same tarp also trapped water and moisture inside. They say that rust never sleeps, and truer words were never spoken. While the steel rusted, the aluminum body panels corroded badly. Four flat tires were the least of it. The original, sturdy steel front crossmember was toast, rusted clear through, with wheels splayed out in two different directions. The interior was in tatters. For some reason, Harry had removed the grill, bumpers, intake manifold, and carburetors and stashed them all either in the trunk or in his cluttered barn. Some pieces were missing altogether, but a lot of key elements were discovered after several foraging trips to the barn.

When I expressed to Leslie that she owned the one missing Cunningham, she answered, 'What do you mean missing ? We knew exactly where it was!' True enough.

The outcome of meeting Leslie and the "yard find" was I became the lucky caretaker of No. 5209. The first step for the car before any rehab began was to literally pick up and deposit it at

Cunningham enthusiast Chuck Schoendorf knew there was one C-3 that went unaccounted for, so he got on the phone and on his computer for months, ultimately discovering the 4th C-3 Vignale coupe built in 1952. It had sat in this backyard for decades, just a few yards from an empty garage. *Chuck Schoendorf*

the 2011 Fairfield County Concours d'Elegance where it took first prize, hands down, in the "Four Wheel Diamond in the Rough Class." A chagrined rival owner was overheard saying 'Did you see how they stuck leaves and dirt on the hood?' Uh, no we didn't. Those leaves were fused to the car.

From Fairfield, the metal remediation began, and the car next appeared at Cunningham Gathering II held at Lime Rock Park, Connecticut, over Labor Day weekend in 2013, where it won the Lucie Cunningham McKinney Award, despite being towed on and off the show field by a golf cart.

Next stop was the epic Cunningham Gathering III that Tom and I staged at the Greenwich Concours d'Elegance in 2018. Major work had been accomplished since 2013, to the point where the car was driven on and off the field, but not much else. For that occasion, the driver's seat was upholstered and one brake drum was plumbed, just in case. Wiring was rudimentary, just enough to start the engine.

Immediately after Greenwich, a major effort was made to rebuild all the systems and turn

No. 5209 into a solid driver. Exactly two years after Greenwich, in June 2020, COVID-19 notwithstanding, the car got registered and hit the road for the first time in more than thirty years. The motor had been rebuilt, new front crossmember installed, plus new steering links, four coil springs, four shocks, brakes, gas tank, exhaust, radiator, all wire harnesses, the interior was completed, and needless to say, new tires and wheels fitted.

All that work made for the beginning of the end. Cars never just go together and run fine right out of the box. In this case, among other things, the new brakes barely stopped the car, a booster had to be added, the tranny defied easy shifting, the fuel line leaked at the tank the first time we fueled up, a control arm catastrophically broke apart, and on and on. But little by little, over hundreds of miles of shakedown drives, it all came together. The final exam was the 4th Annual Catskill Conquest Rally, a reenactment of the 1903 Auto Run, in September, 2020, where the car was the official featured entry. It successfully traveled more than 400 miles without missing a beat."

"OLD CARS ARE STILL OUT THERE, AND THAT'S NO JOKE!" BY JAY LENO AMERICA'S MOST FAMOUS CAR GUY

What's this with all these farmers who have Ferraris in their barns? I've done some research, and farmers make an average annual income of about $42,500. How is it they can afford all these rare old cars? It just doesn't make sense.

My recommendation in finding old cars is to find the oldest gas station in the nicest part of town and ask them about old cars they haven't seen in a long time. You might find something cool like a 1962 Pontiac station wagon or something.

Once my wife and I had to temporarily move out of our house when we had it fumigated. So, we decided to stay at the Beverly Hills Hotel for a few days. I drove up to the hotel's valet stand in my 1909 Baker Electric and the attendee said, "This must be Mrs. Phillips car."

"No, actually it's mine," I said.

"No, Mrs. Phillips has the same car. This must have been hers," he insisted.

You never know what rich people in areas like Beverly Hills or West Palm Beach or San Diego might have buried away because they never throw anything away. In places like New England, like Connecticut, stuff just sits in garages and barns. A lot of it is still there.

I tried to follow up on Mrs. Phillips' Baker, but she had long since passed. But it goes to show that locals might know where old cars are hiding.

I bought a 1971 Porsche 911 T out of a garage at a Beverly Hills apartment building. The original owner parked the car in the basement of his mother's building. He stored it back in the corner and then someone else parked in front of it, so it became blocked. Eventually, the tires went flat and the original owner fell ill, went to the hospital, and passed away. The car was perfect, but sadly the owner was dead.

Sometimes, cars find me. I have always been fascinated with the Pontiac Overhead Cam six-cylinder engine. It was developed because John DeLorean, then head of Pontiac, was enamored with the Jaguar XKE, but all he had was the Firebird. With the exception of the Crosley, whose engines featured overhead cams beginning in 1946, the General Motors OHC six-cylinder was the first U.S.-built overhead cam engine since the Duesenberg. It was pretty ahead of its time [for a US manufacturer]. It had a rubber timing belt instead of a chain, and you could purchase a performance package for it which included a four-barrel carburetor, headers, a hood-mounted tach, and a four-speed transmission.

The problem was the base V-8 engine had 220 horsepower and the hopped up six-cylinder only had 215 horses. Of course, it was lighter and handled better than the V-8, which Europeans would have loved, but Americans not so much.

Why would anyone have bought that car new? Which is what made it rare and intriguing to me. I started to search for a good example, but the couple I found had been six-cylinders from the factory, but then converted to V-8 engines. Then, I got word on one that had never been butchered up. The original owner was in the Navy, who treated it well, and then he sold it to the second owner who sold it to me.

I'm modifying it a little bit to make it a good driver. We installed four-wheel disc brakes, a five-speed Tremec gearbox, a Quadrajet carburetor, and electronic ignition. We're almost done. I drove it a little bit when I first bought it, so I can't wait to see how it drives after the mods.

About twenty-five years ago I went looking for an Aston Martin DB5, like the one that James Bond drove. I followed up a lead on one in Los Angeles that a guy was selling. It had rotted floors and rocker panels, so I offered him $18,500 because it needed a complete and expensive restoration. Later, I felt bad because the guy actually got $125,000 for it. Aston Martins are okay, but I just think of them as Jaguars that have gone to finishing school. I hear there is a guy in the Middle East who is trying to buy up all of them regardless of price.

I've got a 1957 Chrysler Imperial. I got it from the guy who bought it new for his wife. But it was too big for her to drive, so it just sat in their garage for forty-five years. It never was driven very much, maybe 40,000 miles, so the paint and the chrome is still perfect, like brand new. The only thing I did was have it reupholstered because the fabric just cracked when I sat in it.

I stumbled into an amazing collection in Los Angeles. A man, who is ninety-eight-years-old, called me and said he's too old to get around to all the projects he had. "I have a car you should own," he said.

I think this guy was an engineer at The Hughs Aircraft Company and obviously made a good living. He bought a Porsche 904 NEW and still owns it. It only has 900 miles on it. The original tires still hold air. When Porsche needs to do research on 904s, they fly to Los Angeles and inspect this guy's car.

He bought a Lamborghini Miura new, and it has less than 1,000 miles on the odometer. And, he has a collection that includes a couple of ATSs, a few Pegasos, and a Porsche Speedster he bought new. It's just an amazing collection.

Anyway, he had this Talbot-Lago Grand Sport. Only nineteen were built in 1953. This was the missing car. He wanted me to be the next owner. He bought the Talbot in the 1960s during a trip to France. He had it flown to Los Angeles and arranged to have a one-day permit to drive it from the airport to his house in Orange County where it sat for fifty years. After a little work, my guys got it in perfect running condition. The 4.5-liter six-cylinder engine had no compression in the cylinders, so we soaked them for two weeks with a combination of automatic transmission fluid and acetone, and the rings came right back, perfect 115 compression in each cylinder. The engine has the largest Weber carburetors anyone has ever seen, so we believe it was raced.

The owner wanted to sell his entire collection, so a friend of mine bought them all, and I bought the Talbot from him. It's just too nice to restore.

That was a case of the car finding me.

10

THE ACADEMIC
APPROACH

BY GEOFF HACKER

Geoff Hacker, Ph.D., has pursued rare and unusual automobiles for over forty years. He's recognized as the premier researcher, archivist, author, and authority for the history of American handcrafted sports cars. Hacker owns Undiscovered Classics, which finds and restores these rare cars for collectors and museums around the world. Hacker's stewardship of Undiscovered Classics has led to museum exhibitions, special appearances, and multiple showings at prestigious concours including Pebble Beach and Amelia Island. His Undiscovered Classics Team and their cars have appeared on television and been covered extensively in print and electronic media. If Geoff's specialty seems intriguing, I suggest you check out his website: www.undiscoveredclassics.com

Clearly my "driving down the road with my eyes open" method of discovering old cars is in sharp contrast with Geoff's approach. I've asked him to share some of his methods with you.

RESEARCH—THE BARN FIND PATH LESS TRAVELED

My barn find heroes are two people—Tom Cotter and Bill Warner. Reading Tom's first book on the subject, *Cobra in the Barn*, inspired me to pursue a car Tom shared in the book—the *Cheetah Moon Transporter*. And while this was one of my first acquisitions of a handcrafted car, the memory of the process resonates through me today. Here's what the previous owner of the transporter, Jim Degnan, recently shared about his experience working with me:

> "I remember Tom Cotter doing the article and soon after it was published, I was contacted by this dude from Florida who wanted to buy the *Moon*. Six months later, after many late-night phone calls, we struck a deal. He would trade me one of his Renault Gordinis (a car I love) and cash to boot. Karen, my wife, exasperated by our phone calls and discussions about the *Moon Transporter* and the Gordinis said, "Just take the cash and let him keep the damn Renault (Gordini). Needless to say, I now have the Renault, spent the cash, and we are both happy. My wife . . . not so much."

Which leads me to the most important point—no matter how much more I write—it's going to take hard work and persistence to find the car you're looking for. I'll get back to this later.

CASE STUDY: THE CARS I STUDY

The cars I research are what most consider "lost to history." It's a niche part of the hobby—one where individuals or small companies built some wonderfully designed, handcrafted sports cars. I often say that "I search for cars that no one else is looking for." And that's true.

Geoff Hacker calls his outdoor collection of "Specials" *Fiberglass Farms*, where dozens of future projects await restoration or new ownership. The car on the left is a 1955 Byers SR-100, one of twenty-five built. On the right is a 1954 Victress S4, one of twelve built. *Geoff Hacker*

But in my view, everyone should be looking for these same cars. The stories about individual achievement and excellence in building a car are extraordinary. To me, these stories represent the zenith of the car hobby—bringing a dream about an automobile from thought to paper to framework to driving. And doing it with drive, determination, skill, faith, and often very little money.

Our team at Undiscovered Classics celebrates these people by researching their stories and finding their cars. And we have about an eighty percent success rate at finding what we're looking for. Frequently during our research, we find a car with no documented history, which then requires research to unearth its story. So, we're dealing with two sides of the same coin: one side is searching for a car based on our research; the other side is researching history based on a mystery car we have found. Both cases are driven by research, which is the key to my "barn finds."

TOOLS OF THE TRADE

1: Finding the Car—Books and Magazines

Say you read a story in a book or magazine about a car and you want to find the car. Where do you begin?

Let's start with a story of one of my first barn finds. In researching the history of early postwar sports cars, I found references in several books and magazines about a car called the Kurtis-Omohundro Comet. I wanted to learn more.

Further research showed that one car was built in 1947 and another in 1948. The car we wanted to find was the one built in '48. So, the first step was to find the families of the builders. Luckily, both families were easy to find, but this is not always the case.

2: Finding the Families—Web-Based Tools

Magazine articles published in the 1940s and 50s about cars often contained detailed information about the people whom had built them. Full names, addresses, where they worked, and so on are not uncommon. When you have a name, you can use modern Internet search tools even though the information is seemingly ancient.

- PeopleFinders: www.peoplefinders.com
- Intelius: www.intelius.com
- Whitepages: www.whitepages.com

By pulling up information from each of these sites, you can usually identify a location where a family resided for many years (most families from this period stayed close to their hometown and rarely moved far away). These same people-search sites also introduce other family members, identifying names for siblings and younger generations, and those folks are often trackable via social media such as Facebook. You can usually track down a family with just a few hours searching, though it may take a few days or more to get

This fiberglass sports car is a 1952 Alken D2, a sports car based on a very early VW as its base. Cars like this gave car builders Porsche-like performance for a fraction of a price.
Geoff Hacker

a response. How you present yourself is important during your first written or spoken conversation. You must sell yourself before you can buy their car.

Families rarely have the car in question, but often they have clues as to where the car went. Looking for the car in this next location—and the people who owned it—is the next step. If it's a name you're researching, then "wash, rinse, and repeat" the procedure above until you run out of people to research. At that point, it's off to find the car (or what happened to it). Now, your attention is going to focus on "Location."

3: Location—Cars Are Like Fish on a Reef—They Usually Don't Go Far

Neither family had heard or seen the Omohundros since the 1950s. One family thought that at least one car had been destroyed (it turned out not to be the case). Through further research, I tracked both cars from California to Detroit, Michigan—movement that occurred in the 1950s. Then, the trail went cold. So far, that's all I had. But there's still much one can do.

4: Publicity

I had planned to advertise with *Hemmings* regarding my search, changing the ad a bit each month in order to keep it fresh. But before doing that, I worked with Ryan Cochran who runs *The Jalopy Journal*, an excellent

Geoff Hacker's *Fiberglass Farms* was once home to this as-found 1956 Bangert Manta Ray. The car, which sits on a custom chassis, powered by a 283 Chevy engine, has been restored and displayed at the Amelia Island Concours d'Elegance. *Geoff Hacker*

website covering custom and hot rods of the 1950s. We wrote a story on the cars I was looking for and shared history few had seen before. The story ran, seemingly with no luck until we heard from one person: Denise Sheldon.

5: Teamwork

Once you're ready to start searching an area, you rely on tried-and-true methods of car guys and gals around the world. That's what I did when going to the next step in my search for the blue 1948 Kurtis-Omohundro. I contacted Denise Sheldon.

Denise is a car gal from Livonia, Michigan, who saw the story in *The Jalopy Journal* and reached out to me to offer help. Each year, she visits car shows across Michigan, and she offered to hand out flyers with a photo and the history of the car we were searching for. If I haven't said it before, let me share another phrase that's one of my favorites: "Luck is when hard work meets opportunity."

It turned out that the first person she saw was a friend who collected customs and hot rods, and he actually OWNED THE OMOHUNDRO! All of the background work we had done led up to Denise and the flyer— and one of the first she handed out nailed its target squarely in the bullseye.

Another of Hacker's fiberglass "Specials" is this 1952 Glasspar. The car is built on a modified Ford chassis, powered by a flathead V-8 engine and three-speed gearbox. As of this writing, the car is under restoration. *Geoff Hacker*

Denise shared her story April 26, 2008, on *The Jalopy Journal:*

Geoff, I hope you're sitting down for this, kinda too hard to believe and once again proves what a small hot rod world we live in. Dad and I went to the RM auction this morning. Kinda Detroit's version of Barrett-Jackson. Lots of hot rod pals there. I had printed and brought with me a handful of the flyers you sent me. The THIRD pal I gave a flyer to looked at it, pointed to the bottom car and said, "I own that!" I of course said, "WHAT??!!?? are you serious??" He replied "yep, it's in my shop right now."

John had owned it for a number of years. He told me that in 1957 his pal in Westland (next town over from me) bought the car and had it till about 10 years ago when I think John said he bought it from him. He started talking non-stop about the car, telling me all about it blah, blah, blah. Anyway, his name is John Hall, he lives in Saginaw, owns Shadow Rods which is the company that is making those new bodies and flatheads motors. He is just as anxious to talk to you as you are to him. He's never been able to find anyone that had any info regarding the car. I wouldn't be surprised if he calls you tonight when he gets home.

Congrats Geoff! I'm thrilled for you and will continue to look for the owner of the other one.

Regards,

Your Personal Private Eye, Denise

6: Celebration

It's often been said that "life's full of ambiguous victories and nebulous defeats—claim everything as a victory." I started this piece by emphasizing "hard work and persistence." So, if you follow my research-based approach to barn finds, remember to dig in, prepare for hard work, and have fun along the way. And, be sure to celebrate each step. I wish each of you the greatest luck in all of your automotive adventures!

By The Way . . .

In my home office, I have a folder (an inch thick) of one-offs, sports cars, and limited-production handcrafted cars that I've found that are still with their families—hidden away and awaiting acquisition and restoration. Does anyone want to join us at Undiscovered Classics as a volunteer to help extract these cars and tell their story? The Three Rs of what we do—Research, Recovery, and Restoration—is not a bad way to spend some of your time.

Among the dozens of projects awaiting restoration or sale is this 1955 Studebaker Stiletto. Sitting on a modified Studebaker chassis and drivetrain, this car is awaiting restoration, although he has created a rendering of the finished car, on page 160. *Geoff Hacker*

CASE STUDY: THE AD WORKED—FIFTY YEARS LATER

Research drives each of my barn finds. In my previous story, I related my research and discovery of the 1948 Kurtis-Omohundro Comet. For this story, I wasn't looking for a car—I was looking for a story and photos. But lo and behold what did I find during my research but a car that hadn't been out of the garage in over fifty years.

As I've mentioned before, Undiscovered Classics is dedicated to the research, restoration, and preservation of the handcrafted car movement in America. And while if you read our work, you may believe these cars are everywhere to be found—they are not. They are exceedingly rare—especially the nicely built ones.

I compare the process of researching the story of handcrafted cars in America to trying to drink a glass of water by holding a glass sideways and running around the room to collect enough water vapor. It's damn near impossible (actually impossible in the example above). The stories are hard to find and surviving cars are few and far between. That's why I had to get skilled at finding lost cars. And to me, "research" was the answer to getting "skilled."

SPECIAL, fiberglass-bodied 100″ wheelbase rdstr. S-W instruments incl tach, Dayton knockoff wheels, Ford components, T-Bird shift w/OD. Leather upholstery. $1320. Ben Shoemaker, 8133 Milmont St. NW, Massillon, Ohio. TE 2-2288.

SPECIAL, 2-liter modified Bristol engine, 4130 tubular frame, custom aluminum body by Bohman & Sons. Easily converted for road use, weight 1500 lbs. Price $3850. Schmidt, 2901 Coast Hwy, Newport Beach, Calif. LI 8-5533.

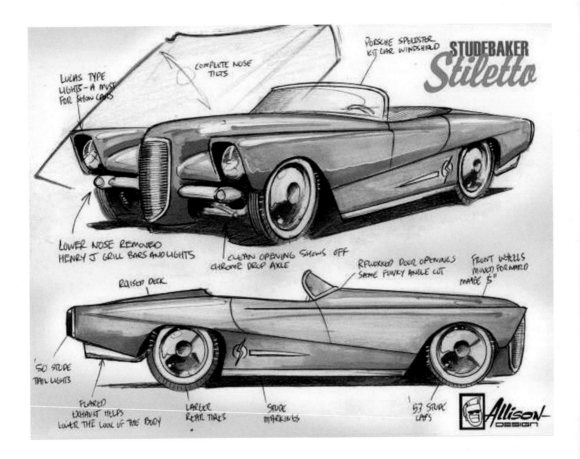

Inside the illustration:
STUDEBAKER Stiletto

LUCAS TYPE LIGHTS - A MUST FOR SHOW CARS

COMPLETE NOSE TILTS

PORSCHE SPEEDSTER KIT CAR WINDSHIELD

LOWER NOSE REMOVED HENRY J GRILL BARS AND LIGHTS

CLEAN OPENING SHOWS OFF CHROME DROP AXLE

REWORKED DOOR OPENINGS SAME FUNKY ANGLE CUT

FRONT WHEELS MOVED FORWARD MADE 5"

RAISED DECK

'50 STUDE TAIL LIGHTS

FLARED EXHAUST HELPS LOWER THE LOOK OF THE BODY

LARGER REAR TIRES

STUDE MARKINGS

'53 STUDE CAPS

Allison DESIGN

Hacker often engages an illustrator to give a finished look to his barn find projects. He then uses these illustrations as an assembly goal for his restorers or presents them to future owners when the car is sold as-is. *Geoff Hacker*

Magazines in the 1950s were a different breed. They captured individual heroism in racing. They told personal stories of achievement. They put you ringside to car builds. And, they had classified ads. Magazines like *Road & Track* and others listed Duesenbergs, Ferraris, Jaguars, and hand built sports cars for sale. And these ads often included photos, names, addresses, and details. If only we could reach back in time. I didn't know this at the time I started my barn finding adventure, but that's exactly what I was about to do.

I'd nearly exhausted tracking down families who have built cars in modern times. So why not try to track down the families who had built cars back in the 1960s or earlier? It would be fun, it would be an adventure, and it would be another way to save history. Little did I know what I would find.

So, I chose my first ad to research. The ad in question was published in the July 1957 issue of *Road & Track* and it was for an Allied Cisitalia coupe. This is a pretty cool car, and I've found some other examples over the years. The company, Atlas Fiber-Glass, Inc., was founded by Bill Burke (father of the belly tank streamliner), Mickey Thompson (of racing fame), and Roy Kinch and operated for about five years.

The car was had been offered for sale by Anthony Spalvieri of Niles, Ohio, so that sounded like a promising place to start. First, his name was unique. Someone named "Jim Smith" would be nearly impossible to find. Second, the town of Niles is a smaller town, so I might be able to find family, friends, and more.

As luck would have it, within a short time, I was on the phone with one Anthony Spalvieri. I assumed that it must be the son of the person who had run the ad in 1957.

Call me Tony," he said. "How can I help?" I explained that I was learning about and sharing stories on the hand built cars of the postwar era and asked if he could help with a car that was in his family back in the 1950s. Tony was happy to help, and I quickly learned that he was not the son of Anthony but actually *the* "Anthony" who wrote the ad back in 1957. How cool is that?

We spent some time talking about the car and how his friend, Hal Thompson, had built it and that Tony had bought it in the mid-1950s. I asked if he had photos of the car we could write a story around, and he said that he did. I then asked if he had any engine photos, and he said "no" but that he could get some photos of the engine if I needed.

I paused for a few seconds. Did he know where the car was? Or was he going to look for photos? I'm rarely at a loss for words, but I quickly gathered my thoughts and said more photos would be great. Then, I asked him where he would get more photos. Tony replied, "It's easy! I'll go and take some more myself. I still have the car, and it's in the same garage it's been in since 1957."

That was something I didn't expect.

Tony and I developed a friendship over the next few years, and I ultimately met and became friends with the car builder, Hal Thompson, too. By 2014, Tony wanted to sell the car. We put together a deal and I traveled to Ohio to take the car out of the garage. Remember, it was in the same garage as shown in the 1957 ad, so we took lots of photos and had a ball that day.

At dinner that night, I surprised Tony and showed him the 1957 ad that had kicked off our journey. He quickly observed, "The ad worked!" I stopped him there and asked him to write that down in marker right on the 1957 issue of *Road & Track* that I brought for the occasion.

Don't ever let anyone tell you that print advertising isn't what it used to be. It's as strong as ever and brought Tony and me together for a car adventure of a lifetime.

I've continued down this research path, and I have met more families, saved and shared more stories, and have continued to build an understanding of the design-and-build-your-own-car phenomenon of the early postwar era. I've discovered more than one car still lingering via the ads in the back of *Road and Track*, *Motor Trend*, and other magazines. I can't collect them all, gang, so I share what I do with all of our Undiscovered Classics brethren. "The Cars Are Out There." Go forth and consider research as a means to find your own special cars. Share your stories so other car guys and gals can enjoy them, too. Who knows, you might inspire a few others out there to become "research barn hunters" too.

11
MY
WILDEST
FINDS

After more than fifty years of bringing hundreds of hidden cars to light, several stand out from the rest. I am proud to share a few of those with you.

BUZZARD'S NEST

The Cadillac was either immediately prewar or postwar, like 1942 or 1946, both of which looked amazingly similar. I was with the car's owner, who had walked me through a patch of South Carolina forest to a ramshackle barn that was open on one end. There, poking out of the open end of the barn, was a huge, black Cadillac sedan, which had obviously been sitting for thirty or forty years, maybe even a half-century. Because it was under cover, the car was in much better condition than if it had been sitting outside in a field. Still, it was one of those cars that would be a better investment as "yard art" than as a restoration project. Even though I was fifty feet away, I could see all the windows had been broken out. They would be expensive to replace.

And the chrome, yards of it in the form of bumpers, grille, doorhandles (inside and out), hubcaps, side trim, and emblems, would cost thousands and thousands of dollars to redo. And we haven't even considered bodywork, paint, upholstery, and mechanicals. Still, for our *Barn Find Hunter* episode purposes, this was an amazing scene.

As I approached the car, I could see skeletons of small animals on the dirt floor. Hmmm, was this some kind of ritualistic animal sacrifice site? Was I next?

Who would have thunk it? The car was surrounded by animal bones and inhabited by buzzards, but I didn't know another resident would greet me when we opened the hood. In reality, the possum was likely more frightened than I was! *Jordan Lewis*

When I looked into the window openings, I was startled by a half-dozen buzzards that had been roosting in the car's interior took wing and quickly escaped the barn. That explained the skeletons.

The Cadillac's interior looked as if buzzards had been living in there for a couple of decades, because they had. Not very tidy birds, I would note.

The owner explained how he had come to own the car, and that he probably would never do anything with it. I agreed that was a good idea. An owner would be financially upside-down with this car in no time.

I asked him if it had an overhead valve or L-Head V-8 engine, and he didn't know. "Let's take a look," he said as he started to fumble with the ornate hood mechanism that likely hadn't been opened since Dwight D. Eisenhower had occupied the White House.

He dug around behind the grille and finally located the lever as I stood next to him.

He worked the primary latch, then the secondary latch, and began to lift the huge, heavy hood that probably measured seven-feet in length. A huge amount of debris fell out as he lifted. The further he lifted the hood, the more straw and leaves fell out, like it was a debris factory. Then, with a final shower of debris, a startled possum came tumbling out as well. He rolled out from under the hood opening, slid down the grill onto the front bumper, and thudded to the ground. Seeing that possum's sharp teeth, I yelled and ran back twenty feet, all captured on video. The possum, seeing the owner and me, along with my Hagerty film crew, took off in the other direction.

Everyone had a good laugh—especially the buzzards.

DOG TALES

"That dog won't bite you," the woman said. "He's as sweet as a pussy cat."

I was glad to hear that because he was chained up near the Ford Falcon Ranchero I wanted to inspect more closely.

"Are you sure?" I asked again.

"He won't bite. He just has a loud bark."

My buddies Brian Barr and photographer Michael Alan Ross were with me as we collected barn finds for our first road trip book, *Barn Find Road Trip*, which had us touring through Virginia, West Virginia, Maryland, and Pennsylvania. This stop was at a little country used car lot in West Virginia.

I approached the Ranchero without much caution. After all, the woman said the dog would not bite. I got to the Falcon at about the same time the dog got to me. As I leaned down to inspect the car's interior, his jaw clamped down on my knee.

I yelped in pain and surprise. Thankfully, I was wearing blue jeans so he was not able to penetrate my skin too deeply. But penetrate he did, right around my kneecap. There was blood and everything.

"Ma'am, your dog just bit me!" I yelled.

"Well, bless his little heart, he's never done anything like that before," she said.

We hightailed it out of there pretty quickly. I had a marathon coming up, and I didn't need to add more complications to an already difficult event.

Beware of owners with shotguns and dogs who "don't bite."

FORD VS. FERRARI

I've found a couple Cobras in my day. I'm not bragging, just stating the fact. Finding something as desirable and popular as a Cobra is not easy. You must always keep your ears open and follow every lead. It's a long and tenuous path that is not guaranteed to end in success. So many people are on the look-out for valuable cars like Cobras that you're never quite sure you've actually bought it until it's sitting in your garage.

Which is why it was so amazing when a Cobra found me. And next to it was a Ferrari. Oh, and there was also a Triumph TR6 and a Morgan Plus 8. It was an amazing day.

It started when I received a call from a gentleman, Warren Cramer, who asked if I could possibly help him move some valuable cars in Charlotte, North Carolina, about twenty miles from where I live. It sounded interesting, so I agreed to help.

Surely, I never would have guessed that just twenty miles from my house in North Carolina were a couple of A-list cars—a Cobra and a Ferrari—that had been parked for forty-two years and inhabited by dozens of mice! *Jordan Lewis*

When I arrived at the house, in a very proper neighborhood, it was covered in overgrown shrubs and trees, virtually invisible from the road. I met Cramer in the driveway, and he told me the story. His friend, Allen, had purchased these cars about forty years earlier when they were reasonably priced. He enjoyed them for a while—and built a new garage for them behind a house he was renovating—but then his life took a turn. As a result, he stopped the home renovations, moved into another neighborhood across town, and turned into a hermit.

We walked up the driveway and opened the garage door. Sitting there in the dim garage was a low mileage red 427 Cobra; a silver Ferrari 275 GTB with a long-nose, alloy body; a Morgan Plus 8 powered by propane gas; and a Triumph TR6 that his friend Allen had purchased new. That's the good news.

The bad news was that the cars had been stored in this filthy, dark garage for four decades, completely uncared-for. The garage had ceiling leaks, broken windows, which allowed vegetation and tree branches to invade the space, and crickets, hundreds of them. It wasn't until I inspected the cars more closely that I discovered they were inhabited with mice. Opening the trunk and glove boxes revealed rodent condominiums.

What a sad sight—some of the most desirable enthusiast cars on the planet, yet sticky and stinky with mouse urine and poop.

Cramer told me that because of the property's shabby condition, both the house and the garage had been condemned by the city of Charlotte and were scheduled to be torn down.

"Would you help me move these cars into a storage facility I've rented?"

He explained that he had spoken to a couple of towing companies about transporting the cars, but because of their rarity, they had turned down the job.

I said sure, and we made an appointment for the following week, which would be just days before the demolition crew was due to arrive.

I engaged my friend Keith Irwin to assist, and we both showed up with our trucks, trailers, ramps, and tie-downs. Oh, and we had on our dirtiest clothes and gloves because of the filthy cars we'd be working around.

Thankfully, Hagerty sent their film crew down to document the cars' unearthing for an episode of *Barn Find Hunter*.

It was a long, tiring, and dirty day, but everything went smoothly. The biggest issue we had was that almost every car had locked-up brakes because of their long, damp hibernation. A couple of the wheels began to roll with a bit of coaxing; others just slid across the concrete floor when being yanked by a trailer winch. A couple of wheels needed to be jacked up on wheel dollies to allow them to be loaded into the trailers.

At the end of exertions, the cars were off-loaded into a clean storage building a couple of towns away, awaiting their fate. It was comical seeing mice exit the cars they had inhabited for who knows how many years and scamper across the floor of the new storage building, probably wondering why their neighborhood had changed!

Cramer told us his friend Allen was in financial straits, and he asked my opinion about the best method to sell the cars, specifically the Cobra and the Ferrari. Owner Allen had decided to keep the Morgan and the Triumph. I told him that rather than us determining their values, we should take them to auction and allow the public to do that. Thus began a long parade of auction representatives visiting Charlotte hoping "to make a deal" to represent the car. Cramer decided on Gooding & Company—Amelia Island would be the venue.

The cars were brought to a restoration shop—not the restore or even clean them—but to start their engines and make the brakes operable.

The cars received a huge amount of pre-auction publicity in magazines and on social media. Walking into the tent, there was a buzz in the air. Clearly lots of people were in attendance solely to see the barn find Cobra and Ferrari.

Bidding was brisk and at the end of the day, the Cobra sold for 1 million dollars and the Ferrari sold for 2.5 million—not a bad payday for Allen, who hopefully ceased to have financial issues. The cars were a relative bargain, especially the Cobra. The purchaser, Shelby collector Peter Klutt, brought a paint meter with him when he inspected the car a day or two before the actual auction. He was satisfied with what he found, but told no one.

At the auction's conclusion, the final bid was Klutt's at $950,000 plus commission. Afterward, he confided to me that the car was probably one of only a couple remaining original-paint 427 Cobras on the planet. "I was prepared to pay 1.4 million for it," he said. "I got the deal of the auction."

Klutt took his new find home to Canada and began a thorough cleaning, carefully wiping away decades of mouse urine, shampooing the carpets, and cleaning and treating the leather seats. Pictures of the car post-auction display a showroom-looking Cobra, certainly one of the finest on the planet.

It's funny how barn find cars don't necessarily need to be purchased straight from barns to still be financial bargains. Sometimes, they can still be deals on the auction stage.

FINDING A CAR DURING A (NEAR) PLANE WRECK

I've always been a fan of Alaska. While in high school, I started having dreams about one day making a trip there, but it took decades to actually make it happen. It's a long and expensive trip to make, and I just never had the cash to consider it until my cousin, Bill Cotter, moved there and invited me to visit. Bill, who grew up in New Hampshire, moved to the Last Frontier to work on the famous pipeline project. After several years of work, by the time that project was completed, Bill had fallen in love with Alaska and had no desire to leave.

He began competing in amateur dogsled races as a hobby, which led to pro races. He won the 1987 Yukon Quest, Alaska's toughest 1,000-mile dog sled race, and he competed in the Iditarod more than twenty times. He invited me to come to the Iditarod as a spectator, which is what brought me to Alaska the first time. I've visited the state four times since: for a total of three times in midwinter and twice in the summer.

(I promise there is a barn find story buried in here somewhere.)

My friend Jack Cassingham joined me for my third winter trip for the Iditarod. We were present for the race's ceremonial start in downtown Anchorage and then planned to travel along the route for several days by renting an air taxi that would fly us to remote locations where we would stay in fishing lodges.

The flight service we employed was called CPA (Christian Pilots Association). Our pilot, Joe, flew Jack and I to a remote outpost called Oafer, which consisted of a couple of sturdy cabins in a very remote environment. Joe landed his four-seater plane, which had skis as landing gear, on the frozen river adjacent to the cabin and taxied to the shore. I'll note that the river made a bend, and that there was a long straightaway on one side and a short straight on the other. Joe landed on the long straight and taxied onto the short section. We had to hike up a steep bank from the river toward the cabin.

Joe waited for us while Jack and I watched the Iditarod teams come and go, and we hung out with my cousin Bill as he fed and cared for his team. At that checkpoint cabin, I noticed a series of long, deep cuts in the timbers around the doors and windows. I asked the owner (who went by the name the "Loafer from Opher") who had chopped at that wood with an axe?

"Oh, those marks weren't made with an axe, those are bear claw marks," he said. "They know there is probably food in the cabin, so they try their best to break in." Yikes.

After Bill and his team of dogs departed the checkpoint a couple of hours later, we told Joe we were ready to leave.

I should tell you that Jack was a jet fighter pilot in Vietnam and is a retired airline captain: first for Braniff, then Piedmont, and finally US Air.

Joe started his engines and idled them to warm up in the twenty-below temperatures. When he was ready, he checked me in the copilot seat and Jack in the back seat to make sure we were belted in properly. Then, he began to taxi out to the middle of the frozen river. To my surprise, he revved the engines and accelerated for takeoff on the short straightaway, not the longer section where he had landed.

As we accelerated across the ice on the plane's skis, we were headed directly toward that cliff we had earlier hiked up. We were probably doing 50 or 60 mph and were committed to the takeoff, but that cliff was staring at us straight ahead. The plane lifted off the frozen lake and started to gain altitude, but not fast enough. I looked behind me and saw that Jack had folded himself into a tight ball, prepared for a crash.

I looked at Joe, worried that he had potentially made the biggest mistake of his life while Jack and I happened to be along for the ride. As the plane gained altitude, it appeared that the landing gear, the skis, would not clear the top of the riverbank. On top of that, there were pine trees that reached another twenty feet into the air. We were screwed.

Have you ever heard the last words that come from a pilot's mouth just before they crash?

I looked over at Joe and heard him say, "Oh, Shit."

I tucked myself into a ball as well and prepared for the impact, imagining what the next day's *Charlotte Observer*'s headline might read: "North Carolina Men Die in Plane Crash in Alaskan Wilderness."

But the impact never happened. We cleared the riverbank and the trees by mere inches.

I wasn't dead.

I turned around and saw Jack lift his head from his tight ball as he gave me a worried little smile.

I looked at Joe. He had obviously seen his life pass before him as well, but didn't want to seem concerned.

"You guys weren't worried, were you?" he asked with a faint grin.

Just then, I looked out the window at the cabin we had just visited, the snowy landscape, and the VW Bus sitting in the forest.

What? A VW Bus? We were probably fifty miles from the nearest road. How in the hell did that get here? Even in my post near-crash state of mind, my heart pounding out of my chest, I noted it as a split-windshield window-van with hubcaps and trim rings and maybe even Deluxe side trim.

A month or so later, I told my cousin Bill about our hair-raising take off from the Opher cabin and asked him what he knew about the VW bus in the woods. He knew nothing about it, but promised to inquire with his friend the "Loafer from Opher."

Loafer called me a few days later and told me he had put that VW on a barge that was traveling up the river one summer day many years earlier. His plan was to cut some roads through the wilderness and use the van for collecting firewood when he visited the cabin. But like the owners of many "lost" vehicles, his dream never quite panned out, and so the bus sits.

BEWARE OF OWNERS WITH SHOTGUNS AND DOGS WHO "DON'T BITE."

12

MY

BIGGEST

SCREWUPS

In barn find hunting, as in life, you can do all your homework, follow up leads, keep our eyes peeled on both sides of the road, and still fail in finding an old car. Conversely, you can do everything wrong and occasionally still stumble on a gem—or get bit by a dog.

To prove that even a blind squirrel occasionally finds an acorn, I share with you some of my less-than-proud moments.

RESPECT THE OWNER

You see a car. You knock on the door.

Don't mess up.

Your first mistake would be to underestimate the car owner's knowledge. I once knocked on the door of a single-wide trailer tucked up in the woods, hidden well off the beaten path. I wasn't quite sure if anybody actually lived there, by the looks of the place. It was ramshackle scattered with stacks of garbage, furniture, and children's toys. But, I wanted to find out about the Corvairs that were lying about.

I knocked on the door, not thinking anyone would actually answer. Certainly, nobody lived in this hovel. But, son of a gun, a man answered the door. He was rumpled and unkempt, much like his home and property.

"Excuse me, I'm curious about the Corvairs in your yard," I said. "Can I look at them?"

"Sure," he said. We spoke for a few minutes, and I noticed the piles of stuff in the house which resembled the outside: newspapers, magazines, and trash. Then, I noticed his big screen TV was on. He was watching the Barrett-Jackson auction! This guy was up on his classic car values!

That taught me a lesson: never assume you are smarter than the car owner. The days of buying an old car from an uneducated, uninformed owner are probably over. With Barrett-Jackson and Mecum auctions airing on live television, eBay available to everybody with a keyboard, and online auction sites like Bring a Trailer, classic car values are at everybody's fingertips.

I think most novice hunters assume they are the only ones who truly know car values, but those days ended with the dawn of the Internet.

CONSIDER YOUR OPTIONS

It was so long ago, I was probably eighteen-years-old and in my senior year in high school. I regularly passed a driveway in which a car was covered by a heavy canvas. It looked kind of low and sporty, but I really had no idea what rested underneath until one day after a heavy wind, the rear corner of the canvas blew back revealing a rocket-shaped taillight.

It was unmistakable; the car was a Corvette, one of the very first.

Of course, I knocked on the door. The owner, a nice guy, came out to the driveway and told me he had owned the car, a 1954, for a long time and it had once been his daily driver. Now, he drove a later-model Corvette, a 1970, which was parked next to the 1954.

"The car still has its original six-cylinder engine and automatic transmission," the owner told me. "But I've been thinking about dropping in a 327 V-8 and a four-speed."

After a little more discussion, he admitted he would rather just sell the car because he now owned a house and had a family. Disposable income was rare.

He offered it to me for $450.

And I had the money, but the following week, I bought a VW Beetle that had big wheels and a bad motor for the same amount.

What was I thinking? A half-century later, I can't remember.

Speaking of Corvettes I didn't buy: I was recently out of high school and working in a print shop in the early 1970s. I had almost zero dollars and drove a Rambler Classic to work. The print shop had a cafeteria for employees. Charlie and Joe owned the cafeteria, nice guys who made real good food.

Charlie was a car guy who was involved with the nearby stock car track, Islip Speedway, home of the Demolition Derby and terrific Modified and Figure 8 racing.

Charlie's home garage held a 1963 Corvette convertible, a beautiful silvery blue four-speed car. It had original paint and he always had the factory-option hardtop mounted on the car.

"Don't you ever use the soft-top, Charlie?" I asked.

"No, it's never been erected," he said. "Come here, look at this."

He lifted up the fiberglass rear deck and showed me the original black top properly stowed in place. And he showed me the original adhesive sticker applied to the top that advised the owner how to clean the top and the vinyl back window. Amazing.

Soon after, Charlie told me he was going to sell the car. He wanted $2,400. I hemmed and hawed trying to decide if I should buy it. I'd have to take a loan. Would it be good as a daily driver? I had no garage at my parent's house, so it would have to sit outside. Plus, it probably got bad fuel mileage . . .

Ultimately, I decided to buy a new 1974 Ford Pinto for $1,995, which allowed me to pursue my dream of road racing. Looking back, it was probably the best choice considering the career in racing management I was able to pursue, but I still have regrets and all seven stages of grief.

Where is that car now? What condition is it in?

SELLER'S REMORSE

Sometimes, you screw up when you DON'T buy a car, and sometimes, you screw up when you sell one.

In the mid-1990s, I saw an ad in the local paper for a 1961 VW Double Cab pickup. The phone number suggested that it was close to my house. When I called the owner, I discovered the truck was only about five miles away. It was a Saturday morning, so I told him I would be right over.

I gave the truck a once-over and took it for a short drive. By the time I got back to his house, a couple of more would-be purchasers were already waiting for my return so they could inspect the VW as well. I sensed that if I didn't

Brian was just a little tyke when I bought this 1961 VW Crew Cab. At the time, its body was as solid as a rock. Ultimately, I sold it to a local guy who swore he would care for it. I never through of it again, until . . . *Tom Cotter*

I was filming new episodes of *Barn Find Hunter* in my hometown and saw a familiar red roof behind a tall fence. Sadly, the highly desirable VW truck had sunk down to the chassis in soft ground. Brian joined me in inspecting our old truck. *Tom Cotter*

make a decision quickly, I would lose the deal. As soon as I pulled back into the driveway, I opened the door and said, "I'll take it."

I could see the disappointed look on the faces of the other hopeful buyers.

As I remember, I paid $900. The truck was extremely sound, one hundred percent complete, and the original 36-horsepower engine ran well. The only rust was in the fold-down side walls on the pickup bed. Otherwise, that baby was solid.

I thought of restoring it and then thought of using it the way it was. A couple of years later, though, I sold it to a local VW enthusiast for about $2,000.

But that's not the barn find story.

More than twenty-years after selling it, I found it again. I was filming an episode of *Barn Find Hunter* near my home in North Carolina, driving my Ford F-150 4X4 pickup, with the camera crew following me. I was driving down a road a few miles from my house when, because I was sitting high in my truck, I was able to see over the top of a fence of a house I had passed hundreds of times.

That faded red roof looked familiar. Could it be?

I pulled over to the side of the road and looked over the fence. It was my old truck!

Thankfully, my camera crew was there to document my rediscovery. I knocked on the door of the house and the owner came to the door. Once I introduced myself, he remembered he had purchased the truck from me more than twenty years earlier. He said I could look at the truck, which he had parked behind a tall stockade fence.

I was sick. The truck, parked in that location probably since he had bought it, had sunken to the chassis in the dirt and was rotten to the core.

He told me I could buy it back if I wanted it, but frankly it was just too far gone. I had too many projects going on to consider another one, especially one this severe.

It was like seeing someone you had a crush on in high school, but over the ensuing decades, they sort of lost their appeal.

13

YOU MUST
SELL
YOURSELF

If I learned anything in my time as a furniture salesman, then a car salesman, it was that you must sell yourself before you can sell anything. Or, in the case of barn finding, buy anything. I believe people like to do business with friends as opposed to strangers. And I seem to be blessed with the ability to inspire trust. I'm not bragging; it's just a talent I seem to possess. At the end of the day, all you truly own in life is your reputation. Sincerity, honesty, and authenticity are traits understood organically by the person you are trying to befriend. Embody those traits and you're halfway there.

When I ran my motorsport public relations and marketing agency, Cotter Group, from the late 1980s to the early 2000s, I had the ability to bring in competitive clients, which is otherwise a no-no in the agency world. In other words, an agency that handled Lowe's could not also work with Home Depot. That makes sense with sensitive company secrets, marketing strategies, and more on the line.

But when I gave my word to a potential client, I was able to sign on competitive businesses. For example, we managed the racing program for McDonald's and for Denny's at the same time. Simultaneously, we had Mercedes-Benz as a client, along with BMW, then Ford, and Dodge. A real shocker was when we were able to attract both UPS and FedEx as clients.

Those clients knew that if I gave my word, there would be a firewall inside the agency between competitive clients. It was gospel.

My long-time friends Michael Alan Ross and Jim Maxwell call it the "Tom Effect"—I am able to put people at ease and gain their trust.

It's no different with old cars. Folks who normally wouldn't open the barn door for people to see their automotive treasures regularly open their doors to me.

My suggestion: Make the car owner feel special, compliment them on their automotive tastes, and ask them about how and why they purchased their car. Too many would-be buyers approach owners with a brusque attitude, deflating the owner's ego and attempting to shame an owner into a sale. In most cases, that approach doesn't work; it's too cut-and-dry, lacks intimacy, and often leads to an abbreviated conversation.

This was particularly apparent when we were told about a junkyard in St. George, Utah, a story I relate a little later in this chapter.

Think of it as diplomacy: that you represent one country and the car owner represents another. A diplomatic solution is when both sides leave the bargaining table feeling they have won. Both sides should leave an automotive bargaining table with the same goal.

THE STORY OF RED'S

When we arrived in St. George, Utah, we didn't have a single lead for an old car. We drove up and down streets for the better part of our first day before we found our first car, a VW Squareback station wagon. After we completed our filming, the owner told us about a junkyard on the outskirts of town

named Red's. "But they've been closed for twenty-five years. You'll never get in there," he said. That sounded like a challenge to me.

Eventually, we found a few other cars, and nearly every time, we'd be told about Red's, usually with a caveat that we'd never be allowed inside. Finally, we decided to see what Red's was all about.

About ten miles from the center of town we came upon a long-closed junkyard, identified as "Red's" from the faded lettering on the door of an old tow truck. The yard encompassed forty-four acres surrounded by a six-foot-tall concrete wall. I stood on the running board of the Woody to get a better view of the treasures contained within the walls. And there was plenty—thousands of cars ranging from the 1950s to the 1970s.

I needed to learn more. I called the phone number on the door of the old tow truck parked inside the wall. It rang and rang, then just beeped. I thought this might be an answering machine, so I left a message.

"Hello, my name is Tom Cotter, and I am visiting St. George from North Carolina. I am driving a 1939 Ford Woody. I have a small film crew with me, and we are here to search for old cars. We don't want to buy them, just find them, film them, and then leave. If you would consider allowing us into your yard, we won't be there long. Thank you." I left my cell phone number and kept my fingers crossed.

How many enthusiasts would give their eyeteeth to own this GTO? Even though it's rough, the car was solid and fairly complete. Though owner "Red" would not entertain sales of his cars for decades, since his passing, his family has put everything on the market. *Jordan Lewis*

THE
"TOM EFFECT"

by Jim Maxwell, MD, Long-Time Friend, Junkyard Dog, and Cobra Coconspirator

To go on an automotive treasure hunting adventure with Tom Cotter is to experience extraordinary observation, wonder, surprise, and most importantly, the delight of getting to meet new kindred spirits of the automotive realm.

Tom knows more about cars than anyone I have ever met. He can spot a 1936 Chevy peeking around the corner of a collapsing barn with eyes in the back of his head while cruising at 60 mph on a country road with the trees in full leaf. I am riding shotgun and fully intent on spotting the next car, and he spots three before I see one. I think it has to do with the fact that he can write backwards as fast as he writes forward, à la Leonardo DaVinci. Have Tom sign a book for you that way. It is worth the price of the book just to watch him do it.

But I digress.

Tom has an odd effect on folks. He totally disarms them from suspicion and lowers their guard with his quick and easy smile and his genuine laugh. They know immediately that he wants to learn about them, first and foremost, and then about their relationship with their car(s). Tom is about people and bringing moments of delight to their lives. Telling their stories to Tom, relating some of the special moments in their lives with their favorite hobby, triggers other memories that involve friends and family.

Tom quickly becomes a good friend with just about everyone and that creates the environment for the "Tom Effect" to blossom.

Tom's love of all things automotive and his love of people is the basis of the Tom Effect. I have personally benefited from the aura of the Effect by having doors opened (literally and figuratively) because Tom is there. Even the *possibility* that Tom is with me as I enter an automotive mausoleum (a junkyard to some . . .) will see the Effect at work because of the aura it emits. "Is Tom with you?" is usually the first question I get, followed by a look of slight disappointment if the answer is "No." I don't mind. I know I am deficient in certain personality traits and knowledge that makes this effect possible. Those are gifts most of us didn't get.

I remember being at one of Tom's renowned Woody Parties and hearing someone say they wanted to be reincarnated as Tom Cotter. Now, for most folks, this would cause the head to swell, but apparently the ego center of Tom's brain never developed properly. This was critical for the Effect to develop.

Another example of the Effect at work occurred when Tom and I visited the Charlotte Autofair a few years ago: We arrived at the Charlotte Motor Speedway along with thousands of other auto enthusiasts, and we were supposed to have passes waiting because Tom was doing a book signing for his then-new Dean Jeffries biography. Well, they weren't at Will Call, so we headed to the executive suites where Tom once had a corner office. After a few minutes, a sweet young woman appeared with passes and escorted us through the bowels of Smith Tower to a waiting golf cart, driving us past the ticket takers and

"The Junkyard Dog Radiologist," Jim Maxwell, has accompanied Tom on numerous barn finding adventures. The two have never failed to lose money on every one of their "this is a no-brainer" automotive investment opportunities. *E. Penelope Sharp Photography*

security guards while fences opened magically for our passage to the heart of the swap meet. The only thing missing was some crackers and caviar and perhaps a bit of smoked salmon with capers. Show staff never even got to check our tickets as the young lady gunned the cart when we got close to the ticket takers, and they just jumped back and waved. I think this must be how Queen Elizabeth feels when she goes for a ride around Hyde Park.

Much can be learned from our past, whether it is from the genealogy of our family tree or for those of us afflicted with an affinity for cars and trucks, via a trip through yesteryear, no better accomplished than by a journey across time and space in a few short hours of communing with kindred spirits of the automotive realm.

If you succeed in making that mental connection with the car owner, you might feel a warmth come over you, not from inside yourself, I think, but from the owners and the cars themselves, the car nuts and the rusting hulks coming alive to say, "Thank you for reviving us." The satisfaction will be immense.

SECRETS OF THE BARN FIND HUNTER

This image seems to have a poetic deeper meaning. I mean, maybe an overweight, gas-guzzling behemoth of a vehicle should be tossed in a recycling bin . . . but in the case of Red's, this is where it was deposited when he was organizing the yard. It was incredibly clean, though. *Jordan Lewis*

Red's seemed to have a disproportionate number of muscle cars on the premises, such as this 1983 Camaro Indy Pace Car edition. Because Utah is arid, cars may have surface rust, but very seldom do they develop severe corrosion. *Jordan Lewis*

Ten o'clock that evening I received a phone call while I was in my hotel room.

"Hello, this is Red," he said. "I saw your Woody today driving around town. If you'd like to come to the yard tomorrow morning at 10 a.m., I'd be glad to let you inside."

I said thank you and I looked forward to meeting him in the morning.

Like clockwork, at 10 a.m. Red was there and opened the gate for us. He said we could go anywhere we wanted in the yard, but he only asked that we not film him. I guess he was shy. He also introduced us to his friend Jim McEune, who volunteered to walk around with us and answer any questions we might have.

Red was a total gentleman and a pleasure to talk with. Jim McEune, a serious car enthusiast, spent hours with us as we trudged the many acres of interesting cars.

At the end of a long day, we said goodbye to Red and Jim and thanked them for their trust and time. And just before we departed, head cameraman Jordan Lewis secretly snapped a single photo of Red's face, a remarkable study of a kind heart, weathered skin, and a life of honest, hard work.

That would normally be the end of the story, except that Jim called me just a couple of weeks later.

"Tom, I have some sad news for you," he said. "Red was found dead this morning in his home. It looks like he had a heart attack." Jim went on to explain that Red's wife had died recently and that gruff old Red probably died of a broken heart.

"He liked you so much and the day you spent in his yard was one of the high points of his life," Jim said. "Your business card was still sitting on his kitchen counter. His only regret was that he didn't allow you to photograph him."

Later, I spoke with Red's daughter, who also told me how much her father enjoyed the day, and that she only wishes a photo of that day existed.

"I have some good news for you," I said. "We have one image of your dad. I will send it to you."

She called after she received my email and was crying with joy. She told me of her father's strict work ethic and how he had built a successful body shop business to later include a towing service and ultimately the junkyard, one of the largest in the state until he had closed it a couple of decades earlier.

I know she had tears in her eyes, and I certainly had them in mine.

Sometimes, owning the car is less important than learning the story.

We agreed that we would not take photos of Red, but my cameraman Jordan Lewis was so intrigued with his face that he snuck this one without Red's knowledge. His family was so happy, that it was used for Red's funeral cards. *Jordan Lewis*

Not a small operation, Red's junkyard consisted of forty-four acres and thousands of cars. Amazingly, local car guys all knew about it, but had never gained access to the yard! *Sandon Voelker*

14
THE BARN FIND
BOOK-SHELF

O f the seventeen or so books I've written, all have been about cars and ten have been about barn finds specifically. It started with *The Cobra in the Barn* and hasn't stopped. The fact that you are holding this book (the 11th barn find book!) in your hands is proof.

My initial fear that nobody would be interested in reading about neglected old cars was for naught. Enthusiasts devour books on barn finds and not just mine. I suspect that even if you are not into hunting for cars specifically, that the adventure of the chase is still entertaining. I suppose it's no different than someone who lives in Manhattan and will never refurbish an old house themselves, but who still enjoys tuning in to *Maine Cabin Masters* or *This Old House*. We all have a desire to step out of our own skin once in a while and do something as outrageous as restore an old house or find and restore an old car.

Here are several of the books I am proud to have written:

CUBA'S CAR CULTURE: CELEBRATING THE ISLAND'S AUTOMOTIVE LOVE AFFAIR

One of my dream barn find hunting trips was with my friend Bill Warner, founder of the Amelia Island Concours d'Elegance. Through an arrangement with the U.S. State Department, we were able to make several trips to Cuba on an Educational Visa.

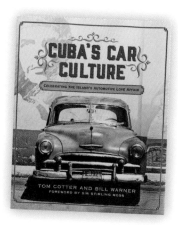

Our "reason" for the trip was to conduct research about the Grands Prix that took place in Cuba in the late 1950s and early 1960s. This was true, because Bill was assembling a class for the Concours consisting of cars that actually competed in those races. But a secondary reason for our visits, of course, was to search for rare cars that were rumored to still inhabit the Island.

As you probably know, Cuba is a Communist country and trade between the United States and Cuba has been banned since 1962. Many of the American cars that were sent there prior to that date are still in daily use. Yes, we wanted to see these cars, but it was the race cars we really hoped to find!

My original plan was to write a book called *Castro's Garage*. I had done some research before we departed for Cuba and discovered that Fidel Castro, Cuba's longtime dictator, was often given cars as gifts from foreign leaders. I figured I'd search for his estate, peak into his garage and report on what cars were stored inside. I imagined lots of limousines, probably Mercedes and Russian brand Chaikas from all eras. I also imagined fancy sports cars with virtually no miles and potentially race cars that might have competed in the several Grands Prix held on the Island in the 1950s and early 1960s. However, as soon as I got off the plane at the Havana airport, I noticed numerous soldiers prominently posted in high visibility locations. These guys were armed with machine guns. I asked our tour guide, Abel, who spoke fluent English, "What if I found Castro's house and peaked inside his garage?"

"Sir, you might find yourself in prison for the rest of your life," he said.

So much for *Castro's Garage*.

Finding old American cars in Cuba is not difficult. Stand on a busy street corner in downtown Havana and you'll see hundreds in just a few minutes. I was told that 60,000 vintage American cars are still in use because there are few new-vehicle alternatives. Many are "modified," having been cut down into convertibles, painted bright colors, and adorned with numerous bolt-on accessories reminiscent of items you could have purchased from a vintage JC Whitney catalogue. Many of the cars are taxis, their owners eager to shuttle tourists on sightseeing rides along the waterfront or into the historic district.

Because Cubans are very poor—on average making the equivalent of twenty dollars a month—the lucky ones inherit a car from their relatives and maintain it for their entire lives before passing it on to the next generation. As my friend Bill said, "In the States, we call [some cars] thirty-footers—cars that look good from a distance but look worse once you get closer than thirty feet away.

"Cars in Cuba are 300-footers," he said. "Any closer than 300 feet and you start seeing the flaws."

This is so true. Soon after we arrived, I pointed out a very pretty, red 1953 Cadillac convertible about three blocks away. We could see the owner was making adjustments to the engine because the hood was open. We decided to go over and take a look.

The good news is that it was a real convertible, not a chopped down coupe or sedan. But the glossy red paint was very flawed. I was later told that Cubans often paint their cars using cotton balls or cloth rags to dab on paint; then, they are "buffed" out with a compound made of toothpaste.

As we walked closer and looked under the hood, we discovered that this was no Caddy V-8. Instead, it was a tiny four-cylinder diesel engine. What? I tried to have a conversation with the car's owner, but he only spoke Spanish and I only speak English.

Later we learned that Belarus had donated tens of thousands of diesel-powered tractors to Cuba decades earlier. As tractors were less necessary than cars, many were eventually stripped, their engines taking root in the engine compartments of numerous large American cars.

On one of our Cuban trips, we had both a driver and our tour guide, Abel. Where did we want to go? We told him we wanted to go to a junkyard.

"What's a junkyard?" he asked innocently. We told him a junkyard is a place where old cars go to their final resting place, and people can buy car parts there.

"Sir, my whole country is a junkyard," he laughed.

Ultimately, we did do research about the Grands Prix races, visiting the hotel where Juan Manuel Fangio was kidnapped before a Grand Prix and held prisoner by pro-Castro loyalists until after the race. Thankfully, his captors were race fans who treated him very well, ultimately releasing him.

We also discovered some cars that had competed in those early races—a couple of Mercedes-Benz 300 SL Gullwing coupes and a 300 SL roadster.

We also found a Healey Silverstone hidden below a pile of waste and parked next to a former Motorama show car, a 1953 Chrysler Ghia.

Sadly, these cars were in terrible condition because of the salty, humid air and the fact that Cubans are forced to cannibalize every part they can just to keep other cars operating. Many of the cars would be restorable if they were in the United States, but cars are not allowed to leave Cuba.

Just before we departed the island, we heard that there was at least one Porsche 550 Spyder in Cuba. We spoke to a man who had seen it at a traffic intersection early one Saturday morning years earlier, but even after four additional trips there, we never could find the car or locate the owner.

MY OTHER BARN FIND TOMES

The Cuba book was unique among my titles, but I'd like to take the opportunity to list the other books I've written. Some of these books are still available from my publisher, Motorbooks, or on Amazon or from your neighborhood independent bookstore. (I am a big supporter of independent booksellers. If you don't mind spending a little more, please consider this option. These businesses operate at a very low profit margin, and every book you buy from them means a lot to the store's owner.) And the books not still available new can be found used on eBay or other sites.

So, in shameless self-promotion, here are the books I have written to date about barn finds:

The Cobra in the Barn: Great Stories of Automotive Archaeology,
    ISBN-13: 9780760319925
The Hemi in the Barn: More Great Stories of Automotive Archaeology,
    ISBN-13: 9780760342985
The Corvette in the Barn: More Great Stories of Automotive Archaeology,
    ISBN-13: 9780760337974
The Vincent in the Barn: Great Stories of Motorcycle Archaeology,
    ISBN-13: 9780760344132
The Harley in the Barn: More Great Tales of Motorcycle Archaeology,
    ISBN-13: 9780760342343
50 Shades of Rust: Barn Finds You Wish You'd Discovered,
    ISBN-13: 9780760345757
Barn Find Road Trip: 3 Guys, 14 Days and 1000 Lost Collector Cars Discovered
    (photography by Michael Alan Ross), ISBN-13: 9780760349403
Route 66 Barn Find Road Trip: Lost Collector Cars Along the Mother Road
    (photography by Michael Alan Ross), ISBN-13: 9780760351703
Motor City Barn Finds: Detroit's Lost Collector Cars
    (photography by Michael Alan Ross), ISBN-13: 9780760352441
Tom Cotter's Best Barn-Find Collector Car Tales,
    ISBN-13: 9780760363034

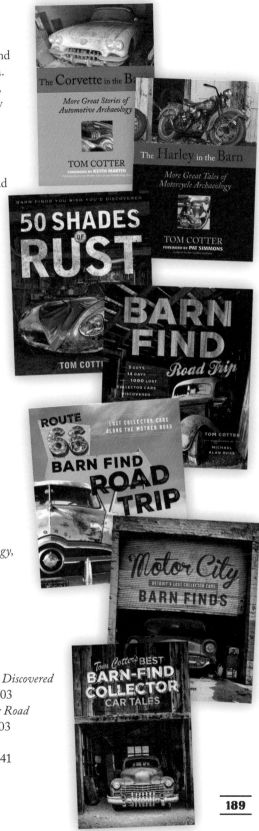

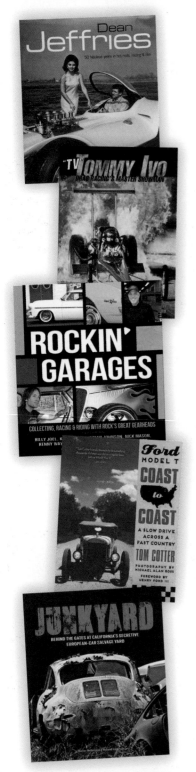

MY OTHER AUTOMOTIVE BOOKS

Holman–Moody: The Legendary Race Team (cowritten with Al Pearce),
  ISBN-13: 9781937747190

Dean Jeffries: 50 Fabulous Years in Hot Rods, Racing & Film,
  ISBN-13: 9780760333464

"TV" Tommy Ivo: Drag Racing's Master Showman,
  ISBN-13: 9780760338926

Rockin' Garages: Collecting, Racing & Riding with Rock's Great Gearheads
  (cowritten with Ken Gross, photography by Michael Alan Ross),
  ISBN-13: 9780760342497

Ford Model T Coast to Coast: A Slow Drive Across a Fast Country
  (photography by Michael Alan Ross), ISBN-13: 9780760359464

BOOKS BY OTHER AUTHORS

Books on barn find hunting have been written by numerous other authors.
It seems *The Cobra in the Barn* opened the floodgates on a new automotive
journalistic category. Some of the books on my shelf include the following:

Roadside Relics: America's Abandoned Automobiles, by Will Sheers,
  ISBN-13: 9780760339848

The Fate of the Sleeping Beauties (Classic Reprint), by Ard op de Weigh,
  Kay Hottendorff, Arnoud op de Weegh, ISBN-13: 9781787113336

Survivor: The Unrestored Collector Car, by Kris Palmer,
  ISBN-13: 9780981727011

Found: The Lives of Interesting Cars & How They Were Discovered,
  a novel by Greg Long, ISBN-13: 9781505388824

Sleeping Beauties USA: Abandoned Classic Cars & Trucks, by Bjoern Marek,
  ISBN-13: 9781845843465

Lost Hot Rods: Remarkable Stories of How They Were Found, by Pat Ganahl,
  ISBN-13: 9781934709221

Exotic Barn Finds: Lamborghini, Ferrari, Porsche, Aston Martin and More,
  by Matt Stone, ISBN-13: 9781613252024

*Muscle Car Barn Finds: Rusty Road Runners, Abandoned AMXs, Crusty
  Camaros and More!,* by Ryan Brutt, ISBN-13: 9780760353592

*Amazing Barn Finds and Roadside Relics: Musty Mustangs,
  Hidden Hudsons, Forgotten Fords, and Other Lost Gems,* by Ryan Brutt,
  ISBN-13: 9780760348079

Lost & Found: More Great Barn Finds & Other Automotive Discoveries,
  by Old Cars Weekly Editors, ISBN-13: 9781440230707

The Corvette Hunter: Kevin Mckay's Greatest Corvette Finds,
  by Tyler Greenblatt , ISBN-13: 9781613253472

Junkyard: Behind the Gates at California's Secretive European–Car Salvage Yard,
  by Roland Löwisch and Dieter Rebmann, ISBN-13: 9780760367681

Still Life with Tatra Wrecks,
  by Vladimir Cetti, ISBN-13: 9788027090990

15

THE BEST OF
BARN FIND HUNTER

Because I had written a number of books on finding old cars, occasionally I had been approached by independent TV producers asking if I would ever consider a television show. After receiving the first couple of calls, I was so excited I could have jumped out of my skin, but nothing ever materialized. Then, I received a call asking if I could come to Discovery Channel's headquarters in Silver Spring, Maryland, for an interview. Discovery airs the automotive shows formerly on the Velocity, now the Motor Trend, network. Sadly, after my visit, I was informed that I was not "dynamic" nor enough of a "character" for their network. I understood this to mean that I did not have enough tattoos, didn't throw tools in fits of anger, and didn't use expletives.

So many conversations, but nothing ever happened with a TV deal, which was fine—I was happy with my book-writing gig.

Then, six years ago, I received I received a phone call from Clair Walters of Hagerty. She asked if I might consider hosting a YouTube video program about barn finding. I explained to her that I had been approached by many TV opportunities, but that I was not enough of a character to host a program. I explained that I didn't want to become someone else just to be on TV. I just wanted to be myself. I told her it probably just wasn't for me.

What Clair said next has changed the course of my life.

"We just want you to be yourself."

With that good news, we decided she and Hagerty's film crew would follow along for a few days while I drove my 1939 Ford Woody on Route 66 for a book I was then writing. Even though we had some hiccups during that first filming, we decided we just might have a unique show concept.

Now, six years later, *Barn Find Hunter* has more than 1.5 million subscribers from around the United States and the world. Initially, I couldn't imagine how YouTube could compete with network television, but now I'm a huge fan. It's really the entertainment format of the future. Rather than waiting for a program episode to air on traditional network television, viewers from every part of the globe can watch any episode of *Barn Find Hunter* at any time, day or night.

Barn Find Hunter began in 2016 with me and a film crew wandering around in the Arizona desert, wondering if we could actually pull off a regular series about finding old cars. Since then, we've filmed well over one hundred episodes, visited twenty-eight states—including Alaska—and even spent a week filming in the United Kingdom. I've added almost 40,000 miles to my trusty costar, Woody, met hundreds of interesting people, and inspected thousands of cars. And one thing I've discovered: no matter if you're from Jacksonville, Florida; Fairbanks, Alaska—or London, England—car people are car people, and they love talking about their rides and collections.

How to and restoration books can deal with cam profiles and suspension settings, but my books and *Barn Find Hunter* episodes have never been very technical. I am a storyteller, and I enjoy sharing engaging human-interest stories with my viewers. I truly love hearing what car people have to say.

Because *Barn Find Hunter* is presented on YouTube, you can watch any episode at any time, even when you can't sleep in the middle of the night.

Here are a few of my favorite human-interest episodes.

EPISODE #6

Meeting a widow who was left a classic Porsche Speedster by her late husband was heartwarming as she shared wedding pictures and told stories about enjoying their sports car as a young couple. Assisting her in selling it allowed her to pay her bills and remain in the family home. A real tear-jerker episode.

(ABOVE) I followed up on a lead about a long-parked Porsche Speedster in Texas. It was an amazing car, and it was an amazing story about a widow who would reluctantly sell her late husband's beloved car in order to pay her bills. It was one of the most satisfying barn finds of my life. *Jordan Lewis*

(RIGHT) Nellie was one of the sweetest people I ever met. She showed me her wedding gown and family photos of fun times with the Speedster. Since her husband's passing, it has sat untouched in the suburban garage. *Jordan Lewis*

Even though Snowball had literally a field full of interesting old Fords, my attention was drawn to this 1937 Ford coupe that he had built into a stock car in the 1960s. Starting out with a Flathead V-8 drivetrain, it was eventually powered by an ex-Richard Petty 440 cubic inch race engine. *Jordan Lewis*

EPISODE #44

(And follow up on Hagerty Redline Rebuild #50)—Retired Virginia stock car racer "Snowball" Bishop invites us to visit his collection of old Fords, from parts cars to restored beauties, plus the 1937 Ford coupe he used to race on local short tracks.

EPISODE #46 & #94

A very private collector, with a dozen buildings of restored classics hidden deep in the woods, invites us to visit his prized collection of Lincolns, Jaguars, Plymouth Superbirds, Big-Block Corvettes, and numerous other cars. He had so many cars that a second episode was necessary to feature "most" of the cars.

EPISODE #34 AND #60

Our adventure to Midland, Texas, yielded one of the best barn find stories about finding, reviving, driving, and donating a 1962 Ford station wagon to McPherson College. In the process, we met a like-minded car guy, Tom Cross.

EPISODE #57

The town of St. George, Utah, contained a long-closed junkyard that we were told contained thousands of 1950s to 1970s cars. "But you'll never get inside because it's owned by a crabby guy," we were told. Well, we gained access and met Red, one of the nicest junkyard owners I've had the pleasure to know.

EPISODE #83 & #84

Barn find hunting in England was an amazing experience, but meeting Bernie, a wheeler-dealer car collector and racer, was certainly a highlight. We were brought to a garage where his niece's Morris Minor convertible had been stored for a couple of decades. Layers of dust and grime revealed a pretty little car that we got running and driving (albeit 5 feet) after a couple of hours wrenching. By the time we left, the car was as clean as a hound's tooth.

People often tell me that it appears that I really enjoy hosting the *Barn Find Hunter* series. It's true, I do; and to me, it's the ultimate compliment when folks mention it.

I feel so fortunate to be able to share with you what I consider an adult form of treasure hunting, the treasures being of the four-wheel variety. As much as I enjoy finding cars, however, I probably enjoy getting to know the owners and hearing their stories even more.

When I first knock on a door, I'm a complete stranger asking about that old car in their driveway, so often, the owner is a bit guarded. But over the course of a few hours—while the camera crew is setting up or taking seemingly endless video of the car's details—the owner and I often bond. That's when the interview becomes magical, and I am often told details that possibly no one has heard before.

Toward the end of the visit, it's often like two old friends saying goodbye and promising to **stay in touch**.

Among at least 100 interesting cars spread throughout numerous barns was this 1959 Cadillac Eldorado Convertible. The car is massive and beautiful. In addition to this black Caddy, in a barn 100 feet away sat another one, but it was red, had factory bucket seats, and tried-power. *Jordan Lewis*

During one of our overseas episodes, a highlight was connecting with my United Kingdom–based racing buddy, Bernie Chodosh. Even though he owns buildings full of interesting cars, mostly American, we had the most fun "discovering" his niece's Morris Minor convertible, which had been stored in a London lock-up for decades. *Ben Woodworth*

16
THE FUTURE OF
BARN
FINDING

Like so many things these days, the very concept of the barn find is in flux. Cars that just a few years ago were considered desirable are no longer as popular, and cars that were recently overlooked now seem to be on everybody's collector-car bucket list. Early Ford V-8s, mid-1950s T-Birds, and MG TDs, some of the most popular cars among enthusiasts for decades, have lost their luster. Possibly, those cars have been overexposed for so many years, but more likely, there just can't be too many unrestored 1932 Fords or 1957 T-Birds remaining. And, there are generational forces in play as well.

Instead, enthusiasts are now salivating to roll up in the only (fill in the blank) vehicle at the local Sunday morning Cars & Coffee gathering. I mean, who wants to have the 20th Anniversary Fox Body Mustang GT in the parking lot?

Cars like Ramblers and other Nashes have become desirable, as have VW Beetles and buses and nearly any pickup truck or station wagon. This current wave of popular cars were all but ignored until relatively recently. You only need watch the results for these vehicles on auction sites like Bring a Trailer to see this trend in action. Enthusiasts want their individuality reflected in the cars they drive. And, not surprisingly, enthusiasts also want to drive the cars they were exposed to and admired when they were younger—same infatuation, different generation. There is a bumper crop of younger enthusiasts just coming of collector age. Volkswagen GTIs, Nissans, Toyotas, Hondas, and any rotary Mazda are in focus and finally being appreciated for being the terrific cars they are. These cars are also more plentiful when compared to cars the hobby heretofore considered "classics," and they are affordable, allowing more players into the game.

"I think younger enthusiasts don't have the patience or desire to perform a nut-and-bolt restoration on a Pierce-Arrow," said Keith Martin, Founder and Publisher of *Sports Car Market* magazine. "They want to hop in and have fun in a car that is easier to live with. Maybe something with air conditioning. And I can't blame them.

"And let's remember that a car built in 1990 is now more than thirty-years-old. And last I looked, a twenty-year-old car qualifies as an antique [according to the Antique Automobile Club of America]."

Let's face it, the Baby Boomer generation (those born between 1946 and 1964 which includes me) at sixty- to eighty-years-old, is getting pretty old. The cars many Boomer enthusiasts grew up admiring were the ones they were exposed to at about twenty-years-old, which was right in the heart of the muscle car era. Conversely, Generation X (1965 to 1980) would likely be most attracted to cars built from the early 1980s to 2000. Millennials (1981 to 1996) would likely aspire to cars in this century, and so on. Events like RADwood and Concours d'Lemons will become the new Hershey and keep "newer" classic cars relevant for the foreseeable future.

"We once had a restored Geo Metro convertible with 100-spoke gold wire wheels [at our show] and it was parked next to a Ferrari F40," said Brad Brownell, cofounder of RADwood. "The Metro got more attention than the Ferrari!"

Brownell's organization hosts automotive-lifestyle events around the country that pay tribute to the vehicles built in the 1980s and 1990s. Participants are encouraged to dress in period clothing (think Disco and New-Wave eras), making this an everyman's Goodwood Revival. Participants typically range from age twenty-five- to fifty-years-old.

"If you own a 944 Porsche, but wouldn't feel right entering it in a Porsche Club event, you can bring it to RADwood and we'll celebrate it," said Brownell.

Consider some of the other changes taking place that impact our evolving hobby:

TOO OLD, TOO SLOW

In the early days of the old car hobby in the 1930s, '40s and '50s, the very oldest cars were sought out as the most desirable. Turn-of-the-century Cadillacs, Oldsmobiles, Locomobiles, Stanley Steamer Cars, and the like were pursued by the earliest collectors and museums. The cars were honored and respected as genuine pieces of automotive history. As those cars became harder to find, Model T Fords became the desirable car because of their popularity, production numbers, serviceability, and ease of obtaining parts. *Hemmings Motor News*, the Bible of the Old Car Hobby, was originally a newsletter for Model T and Model A cars and parts before other years and brands were added.

As rural roads became paved roads and ultimately highways, the earliest classic cars and Model Ts went from being genuine transportation to automotive oddities, usually driven only short distances in parades and during club events.

Postwar enthusiasts aspired to own more powerful cars that could be driven safely at highway speeds on lengthier tours, on vacations, and cross-country. Generationally, more collectors aspired to own and drive cars they could relate to and that they had admired when they had attained driving age.

We are now living through another transition in the car hobby when presentable Model T Fords with older restorations often sell for much less than $10,000. A well-rounded car collection should still have a Model T in its inventory, but seldom does a collection consist solely of various body styles and years of Model Ts, as had been the case in the past. A well-rounded, modern collection will often include a T, but also a BMW 2002 tii, or a Datsun 240Z, or an SS 396 Chevelle.

The automotive universe is now more than 120-years-old, so it only makes sense that a modern collection should include more modern cars.

GRANDDAD'S OLD CAR

If you're of a certain age, say fifties or older, your father likely wanted an old car to restore during nights and weekends, something to drive the family in to Dairy Queen on summer evenings. But as a hard-working man with a family to feed, he never had the money to purchase the Tier-One collector car he had always admired, a Duesenberg or a Ferrari. For the same reason, he could not afford a Tier-Two car, a fuel injected 1957 Chevy Bel Air or a Hemi-powered Road Runner. No, even though he admired those other brands, if dad wanted an old car, he would have to settle for a Tier-Three car, a four-door Plymouth or a nondescript Falcon. "Not that there's anything wrong with that," as Jerry Seinfeld is fond of saying.

So dad bought his Plymouth, a 1936, as a barn find, worked it over, and enjoyed it for years. He would drive to local car shows and parades and of course made numerous trips to Dairy Queen. The entire family enjoyed the experience. But as dad began to age, he was no longer able to service the car. When he got older, he had to turn in his driver's license, and the car was parked in the garage. Eventually, dad went to a nursing home and sadly passed away.

The Plymouth sat in the garage for years, the tires went flat, the battery went dead, and the gas turned to varnish. One day, your brother bought a new boat and decided it needed to be stored indoors, so he pushed the Plymouth out of the garage and into the driveway so his boat could be stored inside the old family garage. Later, when your mother complained that the old car was becoming unsightly in the driveway, it was pushed into the back-yard, first with a cover, then after a strong wind, naked.

Because the car is a Tier Three, demand is not high. And because the car is now eighty-years-old, and collectors are more interested in cars built in the 1960s and 1970s and newer, Dad's old car sits and eventually becomes a barn find again.

This is great news for today's barn find hunters! Purchase of these cars will be easier to negotiate, and they will be less expensive to buy. This will allow more enthusiasts a gateway into old car ownership.

NOBODY WORKS ON JAGS AROUND HERE ANYMORE

In the summertime, my wife, Pat, and I enjoy spending time in our cottage on the Maine Coast, where I spend much time reading, writing books like this, and looking for old cars.

One day, a woman knocked on my door. Her name was Camille.

"I heard you are an old car guy," she said. "My husband has an old car in the garage, a Jaguar. I would like him to sell it, but he wants to keep it. Could you take a look at it and give me your opinion?"

Of course I would!

She gave me their address and a couple of days later, I drove to their home. The garage door was open, and Camille and her husband Richard were doing yard work when I arrived.

When Camille told me they had a Jaguar, I dreamed of an E-Type, or perhaps an XK120 or XK140, my favorite Jag sports cars. But realistically, I knew it was probably an XJ6 sedan, a great car, but troublesome and usually parked long term.

But as I drove into the driveway, I could tell instantly it was an E-Type—a car Enzo Ferrari once called the most beautiful in the world and that racing legend Stirling Moss called "the world's best crumpet catcher."

Richard told me he had purchased it new in 1969 from Hempstead Motors on Long Island. He showed me the original bill of sale, which was still stowed in the console. It showed he paid $5,440, less $1,000 trade-in value for his VW Beetle. He paid $4,440 cash as a twenty-two-year-old. Impressive.

"It was my second car and I always kept it garaged," Richard told me. "But when I moved to Maine in 1974, I parked it here in the garage and it hasn't moved since." The odometer read 44,000 miles.

The car was a Series II with non-covered headlights, white body, red interior, and the original, tight-fitting black convertible top. This was suddenly a great day!

"Camille wants me to sell it because it has sat here for almost fifty years, but I would like to drive it again," he said. "Should I have it restored, drive it, then sell it?"

I explained to Richard that with restoration costs of possibly one hundred dollars per hour, the restoration would quickly add up to more than $100,000 and that the car would likely be valued at less than that amount if sold.

Camille was listening to every word.

"Richard," I said, "You stand to make the most net profit by selling it as is. The moment you begin investing money into it, there is no guarantee you'll get that money back."

I spent some time with Richard looking at the car and then said goodbye, telling him I would ask a few friends what they would pay for the car as-is.

All three Jaguar friends I checked in with said they would pay $25,000 for the car as-is. I called Richard and told him.

"I think I'd like to at least get it running and drive it a little bit before selling it," he said.

Because the car had been sitting since 1974, it would require a complete recommissioning at the very least. Certainly, all the brake hydraulics—calipers, master cylinder, rubber lines, pads, and rotors—would need to be rebuilt or replaced. Ditto for the fuel system: fuel tank, fuel pumps, fuel lines, and carburetors. The engine would also need refreshening, such as oil, filter, and valve adjustment. Hopefully, the rings hadn't compressed, which might require removing the head and pistons, at which point an engine rebuild might be in order.

I told Richard the list of items to make the car road worthy again would likely be in the $20,000 range or four times what he paid for the car in 1969.

I left off saying I would inquire about qualified shops in that area of Maine. The short answer: there are none.

I called a Porsche friend, Ray Ayers, and he confirmed that there are no more British specialty shops in Maine.

"All the guys who know how to work on old British cars have retired or are trying to," Ray said. "They are trying to sell their shops and move to Florida. Maybe there is still someone in Vermont or Massachusetts."

Ultimately, I was able to find a guy in southern Vermont who was a Jaguar specialist and seemed to have the right attitude. Not one of those, "Yeah, we restore all cars. Just bring it in and we'll do it," kind of shops. The shop I recommended to Richard was owned by a gentleman who once owned a large Jaguar restoration shop, but in his retirement years decided to just concentrate on one or two projects at a time.

But all is not lost. I'm on the Advisory Board for McPherson College in McPherson, Kansas. This four-year liberal arts school is the only college in the United States that offers a four-year bachelor's degree in Automotive Restoration. Students must take required liberal arts courses and electives, but they also learn metal shaping, engine machining, upholstery, painting, and other disciplines required in the field of automotive restoration.

In the bigger scope, McPherson is training the next generation of caretakers for the antique car world. These twenty-somethings will literally know how to play the entire keyboard, from Concours restorations on brass-era classics to keeping your 1995 Z/28 Camaro running in tip-top order.

"McPherson offers a starting point for young restorers, but their own curiosity will guide them to concentrate on particular marques, if that's their interest," said Amanda Gutierrez, Vice President of Automotive Restoration at McPherson. "We take their love of the automobile and give them the foundation and vision to become lifelong students, able to tackle almost any automotive challenge on any type of car."

Hopefully, that includes getting long-parked Jaguar E-types back on the road again.

PARTS IS PARTS

With hope for the future labor problem in place, there is then the question of parts. Tom Shaughnessy, a collector, restorer, dealer, and sometime vintage racer said the market for new parts for old cars is being flooded with "pretty parts that don't work." Gone are the days when master mechanics consulted with parts suppliers to develop components that met or exceeded original equipment manufacturer (OEM) specs. Now, an influx of dubious-quality parts manufactured outside the United States with faulty materials land with enthusiasts, and some will fail in short order.

My friend Keith Irwin, who performs much of the work on my own cars, told me that he has installed brand new ignition parts—points, condenser, distributor cap, and rotor—into a customer's car only to find out the car either doesn't run at all or runs worse than when the customer drove it into his shop. Keith, and others in the old car world, have two simple cures: 1) Don't replace parts unless absolutely necessary—rebuild them when possible; and 2) Scour flea markets, online sites, and magazine advertisements for New Old Stock (NOS) bits, whether from the original equipment manufacturer (OEM) or from known, quality aftermarket manufacturers. It's a little more work, yes, but nobody said this hobby was going to be easy.

GOING FORWARD: GREAT NEWS FOR BARN FINDERS!

With electric and self-driving cars on the horizon, where does that leave those of us who worship vintage and classic automobiles? Again, we turn to Keith Martin of *Sports Car Market*: "It all comes back to horses. They were once used for transportation, but with the advent of self-propelled vehicles, horses became an exotic hobby, still very popular today, one hundred years later. There will always be a place and a market to enjoy old cars."

And should a collector want to install an electric motor into their 1956 Chevy Bel Air or 1974 Opel GT, "crate" retrofit kits are being offered by a number of manufacturers, including Ford Motor Company, that will allow you to remove your internal combustion engine and install the latest electric drivetrain.

For those interested in discovering and reviving old cars (remembering that even cars from the 1990s are "old" at this point), I predict we will see the dawn of a new Golden Era of car finding with barn finds potentially as plentiful as during the golden years of a half-century ago. And I believe the same techniques I've spelled out in this book will apply going forward: keep your eyes and ears open and follow up every lead because Barn Finds 2.0 is a time you won't want to miss!

Good luck, and HAPPY HUNTING!

Don't believe that there are no old cars left. I promise you there are plenty of old cars still to be found and probably not too far from where you live. Happy Hunting!
Ben Woodworth

INDEX

TOM COTTER has been involved in numerous automotive and racing industries over his career. Working his way from mechanic and auto salesman to heading the PR department at Charlotte Motor Speedway, Cotter then formed his own racing and automotive PR and marketing agency, Cotter Group. His agency represented top clients in NASCAR, IndyCar/CART, drag racing, and road racing. Cotter has written biographies of the legendary Holman-Moody race team, Tommy Ivo and Dean Jeffries, but he is best known for his series of barn-find books, including *Cobra in the Barn*, *50 Shades of Rust*, and *Barn Find Road Trip*. Cotter appears in The Barn Find Hunter YouTube series, which is sponsored by Hagerty Insurance. He sits on the board of McPherson College's Auto Restoration program and is a member of the Road Racing Driver's Club (RRDC). Cotter lives in Davidson, North Carolina.

McKEEL HAGERTY is a lifelong car lover and the Chief Executive Officer of Hagerty, the world's largest specialty automotive insurance provider. Under his leadership, Hagerty has grown from a local insurance agency operating from his parents' Traverse City, Michigan, basement to a global market leader. In 2017, McKeel broadened the company's mission to growing the car community for future generations. To support those goals, the company has made a series of strategic partnerships, acquisitions, and expansions including the Hagerty Drivers Club, Hagerty YouTube, the Greenwich Concours d'Elegance, and the Amelia Island Concours d'Elegance. His favorite car is his first—a 1967 Porsche 911S that he unearthed from snowbanks behind a barn near his boyhood home and restored with the help of his dad.